Data Visualization Toolkit

Data Visualization Toolkit

Using JavaScript, Rails™, and Postgres to Present Data and Geospatial Information

Barrett Clark

Addison-Wesley

Boston • Columbus • Indianapolis • New York • San Francisco • Amsterdam • Cape Town
Dubai • London • Madrid • Milan • Munich • Paris • Montreal • Toronto • Delhi • Mexico City
São Paulo • Sydney • Hong Kong • Seoul • Singapore • Taipei • Tokyo

For information about buying this title in bulk quantities, or for special sales opportunities (which may include electronic versions; custom cover designs; and content particular to your business, training goals, marketing focus, or branding interests), please contact our corporate sales department at corpsales@pearsoned.com or (800) 382-3419.

For government sales inquiries, please contact governmentsales@pearsoned.com.

For questions about sales outside the U.S., please contact intlcs@pearson.com.

Visit us on the Web: informit.com/aw

Library of Congress Control Number: 2016944665

ISBN-13: 978-0-13-446443-5
ISBN-10: 0-13-446443-5

Text printed in the United States on recycled paper at RR Donnelley in Crawfordsville, Indiana.
1 16

To my children. Never stop exploring and asking questions (even when you wear me out).

Contents

Foreword

I pitched Addison-Wesley on the idea of a *Professional Ruby Series* way back in 2005. As research for this foreword, I dug up the original proposal and looked at the list of titles that I envisioned would make up the series in the future. Wow, what an exercise. Out of a dozen, only one of those original ideas became reality, the fantastic *Design Patterns in Ruby* book by my old friend Russ Olsen. Literally none of the others have seen the light of day, including *Extending Rails into the Enterprise, Behavior Driven Development in Ruby, Software Testing with Ruby,* and *AJAX on Rails.*

Okay, I admit that some of those ideas kind of sucked. However, one of them definitely did not suck and I've been holding out for it since the beginning: *Processing and Displaying Data in Ruby*. The reason is that as series editor, a big part of my job is to make sure that we publish books that stand the test of time. That's no small feat given the accelerating pace of change in technology. But I absolutely know that the need to collect, transform, and intelligently display data is an eternal problem in computing. I was positive that if we published an awesome book covering that topic, it would fill a vital need in the marketplace and sell many copies year after year.

That need was still apparent a few years later when I led a team wrangling terabytes of credit card transaction records using Ruby domain-specific languages at Barclays Bank. It was there for many of my clients at Hashrocket, and it was there in every one of my subsequent start-ups.

The fact is, our world is being systematically flooded by data. Never mind the normal domain datasets for most of the apps we write, it's event data and time-series logging that is really exploding. Not only that, but the looming IoT (Internet of Things) revolution will dramatically increase the amount of information we need to deal with, probably by orders of magnitude. Which means more and more of us will be asked to participate in making sense of that data by transforming and visualizing it in a way that makes sense for stakeholders.

In other words, I've been waiting over ten years for this book and can barely wait any longer! Luckily, Barrett Clark has made that wait worthwhile. He's got over ten years of experience with Ruby on Rails, and the depth of his knowledge shines through in his writing, which I'm glad to report is clear, concise, and confident. There are also three (count 'em) sample applications from which to draw examples—I'm sure that readers who are newer to programming will appreciate the abundance of working code as starting points for their own projects.

This isn't the biggest book in the series, but it covers a lot of ground. I was actually a little worried that it might cover *too much ground* when I first saw the outline. But it works, and as I was able to make my way through the manuscript I realized why. Barrett has been practicing all of this stuff in his day job for many years—Postgres, D3, GIS, all of it! The knowledge in this book is not just pulled together from reference material and blog posts, it's real-world and hard-earned.

Best of all, this book *flows*. Like I did with my own contribution to the series, *The Rails Way*, Barrett has made a noble effort to make the book readable from front to back. Each chapter builds on the previous one, so that by the time you finish it you can go out and land a high-paying job as a Data Specialist! Well, your mileage may vary, but you think I'm joking? Don't tell anyone, but I got my first professional job as a Java programmer back in 1996 after reading *Java in 21 Days*!

Let me know if you try it. And let's see here, let me know if you know anyone that can write some of these series books from my list, especially *Domain Specific Languages in Ruby*. That would be truly epic!

Obie Fernandez
Brooklyn, NY
June 2016

Preface

I love data.

I have spent several years working with a lot of different types of data. Sometimes you control the data collection, and sometimes you have to hunt down the data you need. Sometimes the data is clean and orderly, and sometimes it requires a lot of work to clean it up.

What makes data interesting to me is that each project is different. They each ask something different of you to bring their stories to life. As I worked through these visualizations I was reminded just how many different skills and techniques come into play. Everything is aimed at a singular goal, though—to cut through the clutter and let the data say what it has to say.

That is what this book is about—giving data a voice.

Audience

This book focuses on looking at data from the perspective of a web developer. More specifically, I'll speak from the perspective of a developer writing Ruby on Rails apps.

This book will make use of the following languages and tools:

- Ruby on Rails (Rails 4.2.6)
- jQuery
- D3.js
- Leaflet.js
- PostgreSQL
- PostGIS

Do not worry if you are not too comfortable with something on that list or even anything on the list. I will guide you through the process so that by the end of the book you feel comfortable with all of them.

Organization

I wrote with the intent of each chapter building on the previous chapter. You can see in "Structure and Content" how the sections and chapters are broken up. My goal for readers who want to read the book linearly from cover to cover is that by the end you feel like you have a solid foundation for working with data, including geospatial data.

You could also approach this book from the perspective of wanting to see how to do something. In that case you could look to the Index to find what you are looking for. You could also look at the "Supplementary Materials" to see the commits for the three applications that are built through the course of the book. Feel free to look through the source code and play with it (https://github.com/DataVizToolkit/).

Structure and Content

The book is broken into three parts. In Part I, "ActiveRecord and D3," we use ActiveRecord to retrieve the data we need to implement several different types of charts. This part includes the following chapters:

- **Chapter 1:** D3 and Rails—This first chapter introduces you to the technology stack, takes you through the thought process and steps involved in importing data, and shows you how to build a pie chart using D3.
- **Chapter 2:** Transforming Data with ActiveRecord and D3—This chapter revisits the pie chart to make it interactive, and then walks you through how to build a bar chart, scatter plot, and box plot.
- **Chapter 3:** Working with Time Series Data—This chapter looks at historic weather readings and shows you how to build an interactive multiline chart that displays the maximum and minimum temperatures from a weather station for a year.
- **Chapter 4:** Working with Large Datasets—This chapter discusses working with large data files, how to benchmark Ruby and SQL, and tweaks we can make to gain performance.

Part II, "Using SQL in Rails," gets a little more SQL-centric. We will use window functions, subqueries, and Common Table Expression to retrieve data:

- **Chapter 5:** Window Functions, Subqueries, and Common Table Expression—This chapter begins the discussion of how and when to use raw SQL in your Rails app.
- **Chapter 6:** The Chord Diagram—In this chapter we create a new app for flight departures and build a chord diagram to look at the origin-destination city-pairs for AA flights in 1999.
- **Chapter 7:** Time-Series Aggregates in Postgres—In this chapter we take the flight departure data and convert it from transactional to time-series data to build a timeline diagram.
- **Chapter 8:** Using a Separate Reporting Database—This chapter discusses how to use a separate database or database schema for a reporting database.

In Part III, "Geospatial Rails," we will take a look at the geospatial aspects of the data with PostGIS. We will draw maps with markers, import shapefiles, and query geo data.

- **Chapter 9:** Working with Geospatial Data in Rails—In this chapter you learn geospatial concepts and begin looking at geographic data through the lens of geospatial SQL queries.
- **Chapter 10:** Making Maps with Leaflet and Rails—In this chapter we add maps to all three applications using Leaflet.
- **Chapter 11:** Querying Geospatial Data—In this chapter we talk more about geospatial SQL queries, and I discuss both the "Rails way" and the raw SQL way, to present both options to you so you can choose the one that works best for you.

Appendixes include the following:

- **Appendix A:** Ruby and Rails Setup
- **Appendix B:** Brief Postgres Overview
- **Appendix C:** SQL Joins

Supplementary Materials

Throughout the course of this book we will build three Rails applications. The source code is available so that you verify that you are following along correctly. The applications are broken up as follows:

Maryland Residential Sales

The first app is `residential_sales`. It looks at recent real estate data from the state of Maryland. The repository is available on GitHub at https://github.com/DataVizToolkit/residential_sales.

Chapter 1: D3 and Rails

- Initial setup
- Import residential sales
- Draw the pie chart

Chapter 2: Transforming Data with ActiveRecordand D3

- Legible labels and mouseover effects
- You can function
- Bar chart
- Scatter plot
- Scatter plot revisited
- Box plot

Chapter 5: Window Functions, Subqueries, and Common Table Expression

- Scatter Plot with mortgage pmt
- `row_number()` window function in console (not in app)

Chapter 10: Making Maps with Leaflet and Rails

- Import zip code shapefile and map zip codes
- Choropleth

Chapter 11: Querying Geospatial Data

- Bounding box in console (not in app)
- Items near a point in console (not in app)
- Calculating distance in console (not in app)

NOAA Weather Readings

The second app is `weather`. It looks at historic weather station readings from NOAA. The repository is available on GitHub at https://github.com/DataVizToolkit/weather.

Chapter 3: Working with Time Series Data

- Initial setup
- Weather reading + weather station import
- Line graph
- Chapter 3 tweak 1
- Chapter 3 tweak 2
- Chapter 3 tweak 3
- Chapter 3 tweak 4
- Chapter 3 tweak 5

Chapter 4: Working with Large Datasets

- Import large file via HTTP
- Benchmarking
- Scopes in the `WeatherReading` model
- Add `WeatherReading` index

Chapter 5: Window Functions, Subqueries, and Common Table Expression

- `lead()` window function in console (not in app)
- Subquery, Common Table Expression in console (not in app)
- Common Table Expression + heatmap

Chapter 10: Making Maps with Leaflet and Rails

- Weather stations map

Flight Departures

The third app is `departures`. It looks at historic flight departure data. The repository is available on GitHub at https://github.com/DataVizToolkit/departures.

Chapter 6: The Chord Diagram

- Initial setup
- Import airports and carriers
- Import flight departures
- Add foreign keys to departures

- Chord diagram
- Disjointed city pair chord diagram

Chapter 7: Time-Series Aggregates in Postgres

- Timeline
- Fancy timeline

Chapter 8: Using a Separate Reporting Database

- Create reporting schema
- Scenic gem and materialized view
- Bulk insert into table in reporting schema

Chapter 9: Working with Geospatial Data in Rails

- Add PostGIS to departures app
- Shapefile import and upsert airports

Chapter 10: Making Maps with Leaflet and Rails

- Map California airports
- Airport marker clusters
- Flight path from CEC to BLH

Conventions

Code in this book appears in a `monospaced font`. Code lines that are too wide for the page use the code continuation character (➥) at the beginning of the continuation of the line.

Register your copy of *Data Visualization Toolkit* at informit.com for convenient access to downloads, updates, and corrections as they become available. To start the registration process, go to informit.com/register and log in or create an account. Enter the product ISBN (9780134464435) and click Submit. Once the process is complete, you will find any available bonus content under "Registered Products."

Acknowledgments

The cover of this book has my name on it, but there are so many people who helped directly and indirectly. This is a collection of most of the things I've learned to do with Ruby and data over the years. There have been a handful of people who were particularly instrumental in my becoming the programmer I am today.

First and foremost, I appreciate all the love and support that my wife Allison has given me. I am often distracted by whatever problem I am trying to solve. Thank you for putting up with me, and for being so patient as I worked through this book and also tolerating the travel and conferences.

Many years ago I was a QA analyst. Two women I worked with suggested I become a programmer. I thought that was too hard and that I couldn't possibly do that. Thank you Paula Reidy and Cynthia Belknap for the initial encouragement.

I did eventually start writing more scripts, and then I started making websites. One thing led to another, and I was introduced to Ruby. Thank you Pete Sharum for showing me the Dave Thomas book (*Agile Web Development with Rails*) that changed my life. We've been coworkers twice and friends for a long time. Thank you for being a sounding board while I worked through this book and for helping review it.

I've been lucky to have some great managers who gave me space to learn and entrusted their businesses to my code. I am especially grateful to Curtis Summers for taking a flyer on me when I didn't know GIS and teaching me this wonderful world. Thank you to Mark McSpadden for being so understanding as I wrote this book.

This book was born out of a talk that I gave at RailsConf 2015 in Atlanta. Debra Williams Cauley was in the audience and approached me afterward. Thank you for being there and asking me to undertake this project. I made several new friends at that RailsConf who have enriched my life. It began when Nadia Odunayo replied to a tweet asking if anyone wanted to run. Thank you for becoming my friend and having such great feedback on my talks and on this book.

Speaking of feedback, there are several people who have helped make sure that my thoughts made sense and my words were coherent. Thank you Mary Katherine McKenzie for bringing your energy and perspective to the project. Thank you Chris Zahn for your statistics knowledge and editing prowess. Thank you Joe Merante for double-checking my code. Thanks also to Tiffany Peon for your feedback and for asking great clarifying questions.

When I got into the GIS section I reached out to Emma Grasmeder and Julian Simioni to make sure the foundational GIS concepts were sound. Thank you for not only checking the concepts but also helping make the chapters flow better.

As the deadline drew near I reached out to a few friends to help read select chapters. Thank you Jessica Suttles, Charles Maresh, and Coraline Ada Ehmke for taking chapters at the last minute and providing good feedback. I also had the support of friends throughout the project. Thank you David Czarnecki for talking me through the proposal process and helping me get my bearings when I started writing.

I've met so many wonderful people through the Ruby community. There are so many generous people who are willing to listen and help. I wish I could thank you all personally. I love this community.

Thank you.

About the Author

Barrett Clark has nearly 20 years of experience in software development. He started writing Perl, PHP, and TCL while working at AOL. One day a friend and coworker showed him Ruby, and it changed everything. Ten years later he's still writing (and loving) Ruby.

Barrett learned PostGIS while working at Geoforce, a company that does asset tracking. He currently works at Sabre Labs where he is trying to make meaningful change in the travel industry.

Barrett loves the Ruby community and works to give back to it. He is a conference speaker, mentor, and book club participant.

When Barrett is not writing code or reading about writing code he likes to run and cook. He lives in North Texas with his wife, two teenage boys, and yellow lab.

Part I

ActiveRecord and D3

Data is everywhere. Can you see it?

You have a treasure trove of data in your application and on your server. Knowing how often something happens could be priceless. Looking at the variance in occurrences of something could help you tighten a process or save money on inventory.

Data is everywhere, and if you're not looking at it you're missing out.

Chapter 1
D3 and Rails

Your Rails app generates a lot of data and probably also contains a lot of data. I want to be able to identify and analyze that data, and be able to quickly see what it says—and I want to show you to how to do that too.

Before we jump into all of that, let's first take a step back and look at the various moving parts in a Rails app. These are the tools that you have in your toolbox to wrestle data into meaningful information. There are three key aspects to focus on, so maybe it's more of a three-ring circus, at least at times.

Your Toolbox—A Three-Ring Circus

The three key aspects involve these technologies:

- A database to store and query data (PostgreSQL)
- An application server to broker requests (Rails)
- A JavaScript graphing library (D3)

Database

The default database for development in Rails on your local machine is SQLite, but that's not a database that you would use in production. I prefer to use PostgreSQL in production, as well as in development on my machine. Luckily, you can specify what database you want to use when you create a Rails app.

Why PostgreSQL?

PostgreSQL, or Postgres, is a robust open source relational database. It has flexible data types, including `JSON`, `DATERANGE`, and `ARRAY` (to name a few) in addition to the more standard `CHARACTER VARYING` (`VARCHAR`), `INTEGER`, etc., that enable you to store data easily and with flexibility

Postgres has advanced features, such as window functions, transactions, PL/pgSQL (SQL Procedural Language), and inheritance (yes, like you have in OO programming, but with table definitions). These help you ask interesting and sophisticated questions of the data.

Being open source, Postgres has a user community that adds to, debugs, and generally improves the database. For that reason, Postgres is easily expandable using extensions that the community creates, such as PostGIS for geospatial data, HSTORE for key-value pairs, and DBLINK or `postgres_fdw` for connecting to other databases. We talk more specifically about extensions and PostGIS in Part III, "Geospatial Rails."

Postgres is easy to install. It's the default database that Heroku uses, and Amazon offers Postgres in RDS.

I could go on even more about what makes Postgres so great. It's a fantastic database, and I really enjoy using it. In fact, if you put "postgres is amazing" into the search engine of your choice you'll find lots of tweets and blog posts from other people who are also really excited about Postgres talking about some little nugget that they either just discovered or continue to find valuable in their work.

Database Alternatives

This book will focus on Postgres, but there are other databases of course. A lot of people use MySQL. Larger companies may use Oracle or SQL Server. I've used Rails with MySQL, SQL Server, Sybase, and, of course, Postgres.

There are also non-relational databases, nicknamed *noSQL* such as MongoDB, Cassandra, and Redis to name a few.

Application Server

There are lots of ways to write web apps. I like Rails as a technology and for its community.

Why Rails?

Well, I will give you that there is a fair amount of subjectivity here. I have used Ruby and Ruby on Rails since 2007, so it is something that I feel very comfortable with.

Rails is a framework that gives a programmer a lot of helpers and conveniences. Once you understand the conventions you can get an app up and running quickly. It's also easy to maintain the database with ActiveRecord migrations.

Ruby is an enjoyable language. It was created with developer happiness in mind. I find the Ruby community to be pretty incredible on the whole.

With Ruby and Rails you can write expressive code that reveals the developer's intentions. There is not a lot of boilerplate, and it is not a compiled language. The language gets out of the developer's way, which enables them to solve problems more easily.

App Server Alternatives

There are a lot of other languages. They all have strengths and weaknesses. Ruby is not the fastest language. Compiled languages will be faster. Ruby does not have a strong concurrency model either.

Java is the industry workhorse. Clojure and Scala run on the JVM. Go, Rust, and Elixir are a few other relatively new languages on the scene. They're all a lot of fun, and I recommend taking a look at them at some point.

Graphing Library

I love what Mike Bostock has done and continues to do with D3.

Why D3?

D3 is an incredibly powerful JavaScript library for creating Scalable Vector Graphics (SVG). That's fancy jargon that means you can draw shapes, and they can scale without distortion. D3 enables you to draw any data visualization you can imagine. You're not locked into a handful of stock chart types.

The documentation is very good. There are also hundreds of examples on the D3 website and many more in blogs and on Stack Overflow. That makes it easy to find inspiration and also to learn how to make your own visualizations.

Graphing Library Alternatives

There are other libraries available if you're looking for something simpler or different. NVD3 is built on top of D3. Google Charts, Chart.js, Highcharts and many other applications and libraries also make beautiful charts. Those options tend to have a set of specific charts that you can create. This is different from D3 where you can draw shapes in addition to making charts.

Maryland Residential Sales App

Our first app addresses residential home sales data from the state of Maryland. We will set up a standard Rails app that uses Postgres as the database. We do that using this command:

```
rails new residential_sales --skip-bundle -d postgresql
```

Details on how I set up a Rails app can be found in Appendix A, "Ruby and Rails Setup." Details on getting Postgres set up on your computer (or host server) can be found in Appendix B, "Brief Postgres Overview."

All of the data in this book is freely available from Data.gov. This dataset can be found at: http://catalog.data.gov/dataset/maryland-total-residential-sales-pfa-2012-zipcode-00dc0 or on the Maryland Open Data Portal at https://data.maryland.gov/d/ag7x-nwtv. Download the CSV file. You can also download it directly from the command line using `cURL`:

```
curl -o data.csv https://data.maryland.gov/api/views/ag7x-
➥nwtv/rows.csv?accessType=DOWNLOAD
```

Code Checkpoint

To see the code at this stage, go to https://github.com/DataVizToolkit/residential_sales/tree/ch01.1.

Evaluating Data

Getting clean data is a rare thing. Look at the file to see the following:

- In what format is the data?
  - If you downloaded a CSV file, is the data actually comma-delimited?
  - If the file is JSON I will generally try to prettify the file. This makes it easier to look at the data, and will also tell you if the JSON is valid. The `jq` command-line tool is great for this.
- What are the fields and data types?
  - Do any of the fields have more than one piece of data in them?
  - If you have start and end dates, think about taking advantage of the DATERANGE datatype. You can index DATERANGE and TSRANGE fields with an index that is optimized for that data, and there are also special search operators that make it easy to find the right records based on your date or time needs.
  - If you have geographic data (latitude and longitude) think about whether you will need to do geo queries. If so, plan to use PostGIS. This may have a bearing on your hosting options.
- Do any of the fields contain data that needs to be cleaned?

As a rule I typically avoid modifying data significantly. I want my data to mirror the original source as closely as possible. However, a field may have more than one piece of information in it, or sometimes the formatting won't work, so little tweaks are needed to clean things up. A zip code that begins with a zero and is stored or exported as a number will drop the leading zero, for example. Money may have a dollar sign that we don't want to store in the data. Those are cases where you aren't changing the meaning of the data. You're not creating something new.

Don't create new data. Let the data stand on its own. If you need to add to it, and sometimes you may have multiple sources to tie together, try to let each source have its own voice (database table).

Data Fields

Sometimes you get a data dictionary that defines the fields in the dataset. We don't have one in the Maryland Residential Sales data, so we need to make one. Table 1.1 lists out the headings from the CSV file and also assigns a datatype to the data. The Ruby `Float` datatype is represented as `Double Precision` in Postgres. The Ruby `String` datatype is represented as `Character Varying` in Postgres.

Looking at the data dictionary and the data, I see a few things that need to be tidied up. The field names are inconsistent. I also prefer my database field names to be all lowercase.

Table 1.1 Maryland Residential Sales Data Dictionary

Field	Datatype
`Year`	`Integer`
`Geo Code`	`Character Varying`
`Jurisdictions`	`Character Varying`
`Zipcode`	`Character Varying`
`Tot_Sales`	`Integer`
`MedianValue`	`Double Precision`
`MeanValue`	`Double Precision`
`Sales_insidePFA`	`Double Precision`
`MedVal_inPFA`	`Double Precision`
`MeanValue_inPFA`	`Double Precision`
`Sales_OutPFA`	`Integer`
`MedVal_OutPFA`	`Double Precision`
`Zip Code (Geocoded)`	`Character Varying`

It's idiomatic to use lowercased, snake-cased field names. Snake case means that field names with multiple words are separated with an underscore, like `geo_code`. This enables us to distinguish between keywords, which are in all caps, and field names. You can see an idiomatic example in the following raw SQL query:

```
SELECT field, another_field FROM some_table;
```

We also have some data that needs to be cleaned up a little. We don't want the dollar signs, so we need to strip those out. The data in the `Zipcode` field looks good. Always remember to check those. Zip codes will sometimes be treated as numeric data. When that happens you lose the leading zeros from Eastern zip codes.

The last field looks like a composite field. There are four different pieces of data in that field. We already have a zip code field, so we don't need that again. We also know that these are all Maryland zip codes. So we just need to grab the latitude and the longitude and store them in their own (separate) fields.

Modified Data Dictionary

Now we are ready to think about importing the data into a Rails app. Table 1.2 shows the data dictionary for the fields that we want to create. I included both the Postgres datatype as well as the Ruby datatype because we are about to create a database migration.

The ActiveRecord migration will translate `String` to `Character Varying` and `Float` to `Double Precision`.

The Migration

Now that we know what we want to do with the data we can generate the migration and write the import process. You can find the steps to create the Rails app in Appendix A, "Ruby and Rails Setup."

```
rails generate model sales_figure \
      year:integer geo_code:string jurisdiction:string \
      zipcode:string total_sales:integer median_value:float \
      mean_value:float sales_inside_pfa:integer \
      median_value_in_pfa:float mean_value_in_pfa:float \
      sales_outside_pfa:integer median_value_out_pfa:float \
      mean_value_out_pfa:float latitude:float longitude:float
```

Table 1.2 Maryland Residential Sales Data Dictionary, Take 2

Field	Postgres Datatype	Ruby Datatype
`year`	`Integer`	`Integer`
`geo_code`	`Character Varying`	`String`
`jurisdiction`	`Character Varying`	`String`
`zipcode`	`Character Varying`	`String`
`total_sales`	`Integer`	`Integer`
`median_value`	`Double Precision`	`Float`
`mean_value`	`Double Precision`	`Float`
`sales_inside_pfa`	`Double Precision`	`Float`
`median_value_in_pfa`	`Double Precision`	`Float`
`mean_value_in_pfa`	`Double Precision`	`Float`
`sales_outside_pfa`	`Integer`	`Integer`
`median_value_out_pfa`	`Double Precision`	`Float`
`mean_value_out_pfa`	`Character Varying`	`String`
`latitude`	`Double Precision`	`Float`
`longitude`	`Double Precision`	`Float`

The backslash at the end of each line in that command is how we tell the Unix command line that a command continues on the next line.

I usually include the `--pretend` switch at the end whenever I initially run a generator so that I can see what it thinks it needs to create and also whether there will be any errors. If you're new to Rails, take a look at the files that are created.

When you are ready to create the table you can run the database migrations with `bundle exec rake db:migrate`.

Custom Rake Task

Rake is a build tool for Ruby. It can help us streamline tedious or repetitive tasks. You can use rake in any Ruby project, and Rails ships with several tasks available to you. You can also write your own rake tasks.

I like to create rake tasks in the `db:seed` namespace for importing data, such as `db:seed:import_foo`. This is an action that will load (seed) the database with the data from this file, so it makes sense to me for it to be in the `db:seed` namespace.

The following line shows the generator command to create the shell of a new rake task.

```
rails generate task seed import_maryland_residential_sales
```

That adds a file at `lib/tasks/seeds.rake` and gives you a task in the `seed` namespace, but we want that nested inside the `db` namespace. We need to update the new rake task manually. You can see the updated code in the following snippet.

```
namespace :db do
  namespace :seed do
    desc "TODO"
    task import_maryland_residential_sales: :environment do
    end
  end
end
```

Writing the ETL

ETL stands for Extract, Transform, Load. In this case, we have a file, so the data has already been extracted. We need to transform the data to clean it up as we identified earlier in this section, and we need to load it into the database. Listing 1.1 shows the full rake task to import the Maryland Residential Sales data.

I like what Avdi Grimm advocates in *Confident Ruby* for type checking and error handling. We don't want to accidentally coerce an invalid value to `0`, like we would if we called `to_i`, so instead we use `Kernel#Integer`. That way we get an exception when the data is invalid, and we can figure out what to do from there rather than accidentally load bad data without knowing. That is a bad lesson to learn the hard way.

You'll also note that this expects there to be a file in the `db/data_files` directory, which you can create now and move the CSV file into. If the data file is too big or if you don't want to have it in the repo you can also store it in S3 or stream it from the original source. I'll discuss this strategy more in Chapter 4, "Working with Large Datasets."

Also note that none of the transform logic lives in the `SalesFigure` model. This is not business logic that the app will depend on. There's no need to clutter up the object model with it.

Listing 1.1 Completed Maryland Residential Sales Import Rake Task

```
require 'csv'
namespace :db do
  namespace :seed do
    desc "Import Maryland Residential Sales CSV"
    task :import_maryland_residential_sales => :environment do
      def float(string)
        return nil if string.nil?
        Float(string.sub(/\$/, ''))
```

```
      end

      filename = File.join(Rails.root, 'db', 'data_files','data.csv')
      CSV.foreach(filename, :headers => true) do |row|
        puts $. if $. % 10000 == 0
        regex  = /.*(\d{2}\.\d*), (-\d{2}\.\d*).*/
        latlng = row['Zip Code (Geocoded)'].match(regex)
        values = {
          :year                 => row['Year'],
          :geo_code             => row['Geo Code'],
          :jurisdiction         => row['Jurisdictions'],
          :zipcode              => row['Zipcode'],
          :total_sales          => Integer(row['Tot_Sales']),
          :median_value         => float(row['MedianValue']),
          :mean_value           => float(row['MeanValue']),
          :sales_inside_pfa     => row['Sales_insidePFA'],
          :median_value_in_pfa  => float(row['MedVal_inPFA']),
          :mean_value_in_pfa    => float(row['MeanVal_inPFA']),
          :sales_outside_pfa    => float(row['Sales_OutPFA']),
          :median_value_out_pfa => float(row['MedVal_OutPFA']),
          :mean_value_out_pfa   => float(row['MeanVal_OutPFA']),
          :latitude             => float(latlng[1]),
          :longitude            => float(latlng[2])
        }
        SalesFigure.create(values)
      end
    end
  end
end
```

Don't be scared by the regular expression or the match. Here's how that works.

```
>> zipcoded = "Maryland 21502 (39.64, -78.77)"
=> "Maryland 21502 (39.64, -78.77)"
>> latlng = zipcoded.match(/.*(\d{2}\.\d*), (-\d{2}\.\d*).*/)
=> #<MatchData "Maryland 21502 (39.64, -78.77)" 1:"39.64" 2:"-78.77">
>> latlng[1]
=> "39.64"
```

In the regex we create two buffers with one for the latitude and one for the longitude. The match just looks for that pattern in the string. If it finds the pattern, it returns the match and exposes the buffers (1, 2, 3... n). You access those buffers by their buffer number. The latitude is in the first buffer, so it's `latlng[1]`. The full string parsed by the regex is available in `latlng[0]`.

Now run the task from the command line:

```
bundle exec rake db:seed:import_maryland_residential_sales
```

Logging

Visibility is a good thing. Look at any logs automatically generated. I like to make sure there are no errors first and foremost. I also like to see what is executed. For example, I like to see what SQL is generated by ActiveRecord and how long it takes to execute. For any web request you can see how long the total response took, and how long each component of the request took. The database and view generation times are both broken out and the total request time is also logged.

You can also log your own output. In a Rails app you can log to the Rails log file using the `Rails.logger` command. Using `puts` will print to `STDOUT` rather than to a log file. This is beneficial in local development, but you won't be able to see that when you deploy to Heroku and run the task there. Learn more at http://guides.rubyonrails.org/debugging_rails_applications.html.

Alternative Ways to Import Data

Importing a file record-by-record using ActiveRecord is convenient, but it's also resource expensive.

You can also use the Postgres `COPY` or `\copy` commands. This does a bulk import of the data, so the data needs to be clean and have the same fields as the destination table. You may have to create an import-friendly version of the data file.

Do note that `COPY` and `\copy` are different. From the Postgres documentation:

> Files named in a COPY command are read or written directly by the server, not by the client application. Therefore, they must reside on or be accessible to the database server machine, not the client. They must be accessible to and readable or writable by the PostgreSQL user (the user ID the server runs as), not the client. COPY naming a file is only allowed to database superusers, since it allows reading or writing any file that the server has privileges to access.
>
> Do not confuse COPY with the psql instruction \copy. \copy invokes COPY FROM STDIN or COPY TO STDOUT, and then fetches/stores the data in a file accessible to the psql client. Thus, file accessibility and access rights depend on the client rather than the server when \copy is used.

In other words, you can use `COPY` on your localhost or when you have shell access to the database server. Otherwise you have to use `\copy` from the command line of your host. To do this in production you would typically write a script or shell out to the command, and you would have to have the Postgresql client library installed.

I talk more about bulk importing in Appendix B.

Confirm the Data

Log into the database or use Rails console to look at the imported data to make sure that there were no error messages or issues with data being converted incorrectly. If there were, you can drop the table (or rerun the migration) and rerun the import task. Listing 1.2 shows an example of fetching the first record and printing it out using Ruby's pretty print (`pp`) command. You can see in the first line that we can enter the Rails console by typing `rails c` from the command line. The Rails console is an enhanced version of Ruby's `irb` REPL with the Rails app's environment loaded.

If you have not seen the `; nil` at the end of the statement before, that's a way to have the statement return `nil` rather than the object, so that you don't get the unformatted version of the object in addition to the pretty printed version.

Listing 1.2 Confirming the Imported Data from Rails Console

```
$ rails console
>> pp SalesFigure.first; nil
  SalesFigure Load (0.6ms)  SELECT
➥"maryland_residential_sales_figures".* FROM
➥"maryland_residential_sales_figures"  ORDER BY
➥"maryland_residential_sales_figures"."id" ASC LIMIT 1
#<SalesFigure:0x007fd2c47b0a68
 id: 1,
 year: 2012,
 geo_code: nil,
 jurisdiction: "Allegany",
 zipcode: "21502",
 total_sales: 175,
 median_value: 98242.0,
 mean_value: 111950.0,
 sales_inside_pfa: 172,
 median_value_in_pfa: 97250.0,
 mean_value_in_pfa: nil,
 sales_outside_pfa: 3,
 median_value_out_pfa: 999.0,
 mean_value_out_pfa: 999.0,
 latitude: 39.6476079090005,
 longitude: -78.7730260849996,
 created_at: Fri, 11 Sep 2015 17:25:02 UTC +00:00,
 updated_at: Fri, 11 Sep 2015 17:25:02 UTC +00:00>
=> nil
```

I also like to run a count on the table to make sure it lines up with what I expected to be imported. You can use `wc -l` on the command line to get the number of lines in a file. Subtract one if there is a header row in the file.

Code Checkpoint

To see the code at this stage, go to https://github.com/DataVizToolkit/residential_sales/tree/ch01.2.

Simple Pie Chart

Now that we have some data, let's see what it *really* looks like—visually. To do that we need to create a view and write a little bit of JavaScript.

Including the D3 JavaScript Library

There are a handful of ways to include a JavaScript file or library in a Rails app.

- You can download the source and put it in `app/assets/javascripts` or `app/vendor/javascripts`, then reference it in your layout or template, or include it in your `application.js` file.
- You can use Bower or Gulp to manage front-end dependencies.
- Sometimes there is a gem available that wraps up a library. Rails includes the `jquery-rails` gem to give us the jQuery source, for example. There is also a gem available for the D3 source: `d3-rails`.
- You can link to a CDN in your application layout or a specified template. This is my preferred method.

Add the following line to your `app/views/layouts/application.html.erb` file above the `javascript_include_tag` for application:

```
<%= javascript_include_tag
➥'https://cdnjs.cloudflare.com/ajax/libs/d3/3.5.17/d3.min.js' %>
```

The Residential View

With the help from the Rails generators we can quickly and easily create the pieces that we need to make our first pie chart. In the following we use the Rails generator to create a controller with a single action that will correspond to our "view."

```
rails g controller residential index
```

That will give you the controller, route, and view files that you need to serve an index page. Delete the placeholder text in `app/views/residential/index.html.erb`. This file can be completely empty. We are going to generate the content with JavaScript!

And speaking of the JavaScript, we need to add another route for the script to request the data we need for the pie chart. Manually add another route, so that `config/routes.rb` looks like this:

```
Rails.application.routes.draw do
  get 'residential/index'
  get 'residential/data', :defaults => { :format => 'json' }
  root :to => 'residential#index'
end
```

I deleted all the example routes from my version, but it doesn't hurt anything to leave them in. I also like to define the `root` route to be whatever makes the most sense. In this case it is the residential `index` action.

The last view-related thing we need to do is add some CSS to style the pie chart. Place this code in `app/assets/stylesheets/residential.scss`:

```
.arc text {
  font: 10px sans-serif;
  text-anchor: middle;
}

.arc path {
  stroke: #fff;
}
```

The Residential Controller

We just deleted everything from the view, so it doesn't require that we do anything in the controller for the `index` action. We will make a separate AJAX call to get the data, which is why we added the `residential/data` route.

We will use ActiveRecord to pull the data and group it by jurisdiction (county) so that we can get the sum of the `total_sales` field by county.

Here is the controller:

```
class ResidentialController < ApplicationController
  def index
  end

  def data
    totals = SalesFigure.group(:jurisdiction).sum(:total_sales)
    render :json => { :totals => totals }
  end
end
```

The data action asks the database for the sum of the `total_sales` column, and it wants that sum grouped by `jurisdiction`. In other words, we ask the database for the total sales by county. The SQL generated by that ActiveRecord grouping and calculation will look something like this:

```
SELECT SUM("maryland_residential_sales_figures"."total_sales") AS sum_total_sales,
  jurisdiction AS jurisdiction
FROM "maryland_residential_sales_figures"
GROUP BY "maryland_residential_sales_figures"."jurisdiction"
```

Pie Chart JavaScript

Now all we have to do is write a little bit of D3-flavored JavaScript. Mike Bostock, the creator of D3, has created hundreds of examples to draw inspiration from. I grabbed the example in Listing 1.3 from http://bl.ocks.org/mbostock/3887235.

You'll note that this is written in JavaScript rather than CoffeeScript. You can rename any file that Rails creates with a `.coffee` extension to have a `.js` extension. I put this code in `app/assets/javascripts/residential.js`.

Listing 1.3 Pie Chart

```
$(function() {
  // From: http://bl.ocks.org/mbostock/3887235
  // Set the dimensions
  var width  = 960,
      height = 500,
      radius = Math.min(width, height) / 2;

  var totals = {};
  var color  = d3.scale.category20b();

  // This is the circle that the pie will fill in
  var arc = d3.svg.arc()
      .outerRadius(radius - 10)
      .innerRadius(0);

  // D3 provides a helper function for creating the pie and slices
  var pie = d3.layout.pie()
      .sort(null)
      .value(function(d) { return totals[d]; });

  // Add an SVG element to the page and append a G element for the pie
  var svg = d3.select("body").append("svg")
      .attr("width", width)
      .attr("height", height)
    .append("g")
      .attr("transform", "translate(" + width / 2 + "," + height / 2 +
➥")");
```

```
  // Get the data and draw the slices
  $.getJSON('/residential/data', function(data) {
    totals = data.totals;
    // enter is how we tell D3 to generate the SVG elements for the data
    var g = svg.selectAll(".arc")
        .data(pie(d3.keys(totals)))
      .enter().append("g")
        .attr("class", "arc");

    // color the pie slices using the color pallet
    g.append("path")
        .attr("d", arc)
        .style("fill", function(d) { return color(d.data); });

    // add the jurisdiction name
    g.append("text")
      .attr("transform", function(d) {
        return "translate(" + arc.centroid(d) + ")";
       })
      .attr("dy", ".35em")
      .style("text-anchor", "middle")
      .text(function(d) { return d.data; });
  });
});
```

Ship It

If everything goes according to plan, when you run the server and go to http://localhost:3000 you will be able to marvel at your amazing pie chart, which you can also see in Figure 1.1.

OK, so maybe it's not "amazing" but it's a starting point.

Code Checkpoint

To see the code at this stage, go to https://github.com/DataVizToolkit/residential_sales/tree/ch01.3.

Summary

We covered a lot of ground in this first chapter. Good, clean data is fundamentally important. Taking the time to understand your data and work around the limitations that it brings with it will save you an immense amount of frustration later.

This chapter was focused on giving you a taste of the three key components of a Rails data visualization app: the database, the Rails app, and D3. Refer to Appendix A for

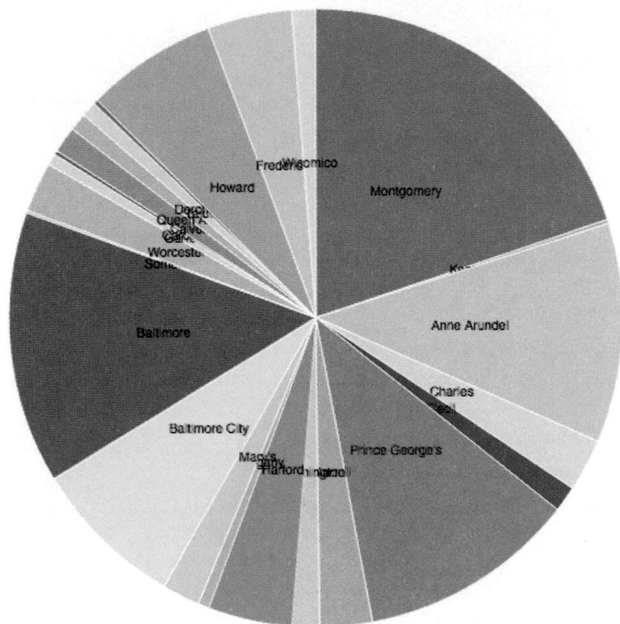

Figure 1.1 First Pie Chart

more information on setting up your Rails environment, and Appendix B for more information on setting up Postgres.

We created our first Rails app and loaded a data file. We also created our first visualization—a pie chart that shows the total sales by county for home sales in Maryland.

The next chapter will dig even deeper into more visualizations.

CHAPTER 2

Transforming Data with ActiveRecord and D3

There are so many good examples of D3 charts ranging from very simple to very intricate. My typical workflow is to find an existing example that does generally what I am looking for and use that as my foundation or inspiration. That's what we did in the previous chapter.

Once I have the data lined up and the graph in place I can start tweaking it. That's exactly what we are going to do with the simple pie chart we made in the previous chapter.

Pie Chart Revisited

The labels in our pie chart are a bit jumbled. We have a lot more slices in our pie than the example, and there are too many slices that are small and have similar colors. It is not very clear at a glance exactly what the chart is saying. We need to do something to make our chart as useful as possible.

Legible Labels

I would prefer to have all the labels visible in or near the pie slices. I want to avoid having a legend with 24 items in it for this pie chart. That would be a big legend that would steal focus from the chart itself.

We can move the labels outside the pie chart fairly easily, and we can even highlight a slice (and its label) when you hover over the slice with your mouse. That's pretty helpful. If you wanted to go even further you could add a tooltip that appears and gives even more information, but we are going to hold off on that for now.

In the section of the JavaScript where we add the labels (inside the `$.getJSON` block toward the bottom) we need to create another arc outside the existing arc that we've drawn for the pie chart. Attach the label to the new arc rather than the pie chart's arc. We do that by replacing the existing label creation code with the following:

```
// put the labels outside the pie (in a new arc/circle)
var pos = d3.svg.arc().innerRadius(radius + 20).outerRadius(radius + 20);
g.append("text")
    .attr("transform", function(d) {
      return "translate(" + pos.centroid(d) + ")";
    })
    .attr("dy", ".35em")
    .style("text-anchor", "middle")
    .text(function(d) { return d.data; });
```

Admittedly, it is a very naive implementation. Also, notice that it causes some of the labels to be cut off at the bottom of the canvas. We'll handle that later. The labels are still a bit jumbled. We could add some collision detection, and having lines that connect the label to the slice would probably be where I would want to go next with this. There is definitely still room for improvement.

For now, we are going to stick with the simpler implementation. We aren't really sure that this pie chart is even the visualization that we really want for this data yet.

Beware of Misleading Charts

It should be very clear at a glance what your chart is communicating. You can use graphs in very deceptive ways. You may see this especially in the political arena. Adding 3D effects and cutouts can make it difficult to discern the details. Pie charts are bad at communicating finer details, too. Can you visibly see the difference between 20% and 30% slices? Clear labels can transform a pie chart from "cute picture" to "useful visualization." You should always have clearly labeled axes. Truncating an axis, or having too many axes will generally add confusion to your graph.

Mouseover Effects

One last thing that we can do with the slices and labels to help them stand out is to add some mouseover effects. Adding an effect to the pie slice is as easy as adding a little CSS to `app/assets/stylesheets/residential.scss`.

```
g.arc {
  &:hover {
    opacity: .55;
```

```
  }
}
```

With the CSS in place you can see that the opacity of the pie pieces changes as you move the mouse around the pie chart.

To make the label stand out I want to make the text a little larger. To do that we add some `mouseover` and `mouseout` event handlers to the section of the function where we generate the pie slices. The bold part is the new code.

```
// make each pie piece
var g = svg.selectAll(".arc")
    .data(pie(d3.keys(totals)))
  .enter().append("g")
    .attr("class", "arc")
  .on("mouseover", function(d) {
    d3.select(this).select("text").style("font-weight", "bold")
    d3.select(this).select("text").style("font-size", "1.25em")
  })
  .on("mouseout", function(d) {
    d3.select(this).select("text").style("font-weight", "normal")
    d3.select(this).select("text").style("font-size", "1em")
  })
;
```

With those two tweaks you will now see the color fade a little for each slice as you hover, and the label will also stand out a little more.

As you hover around you may see the labels do not return to their original size. We can tell the page what `1em` means by setting the font size for the body. Simply add `"body, "` before `.arc text` at the beginning of `app/stylesheets/residential`.scss to also apply the style to the `body`.

Code Checkpoint

To see the code at this stage, go to https://github.com/DataVizToolkit/residential_sales/tree/ch02.1.

You Can Function

There is one last change that we need to make before we can move on from this pie chart example. The code to generate the chart is sitting in the open on the global scope. When the main document is ready, all the JavaScript on the global scope will be called. That's not what we want. We want the view to decide when it is ready to ask for a chart and which chart it wants to ask for.

We need to wrap the JavaScript in a function of its own, and we need to update the view to ask for that function. The function does not need to take any parameters, so let's just call it `makePie`, and then we have the view ask for `makePie()` when the page has loaded. You can see the final `index.html.erb` in the next listing.

The final version of the pie chart can be seen in Figure 2.1.

```
<!-- A pie chart will magically appear here -->
<script>
$(document).on('ready page:load', function(event) {
  // apply non-idempotent transformations to the body
  makePie();
});
</script>
```

The final JavaScript to render the pie chart is shown in Listing 2.1.

Listing 2.1 Final **`makePie()`** JavaScript

```
function makePie() {
  // From: http://bl.ocks.org/mbostock/3887235
  // Start by defining some basic variables
```

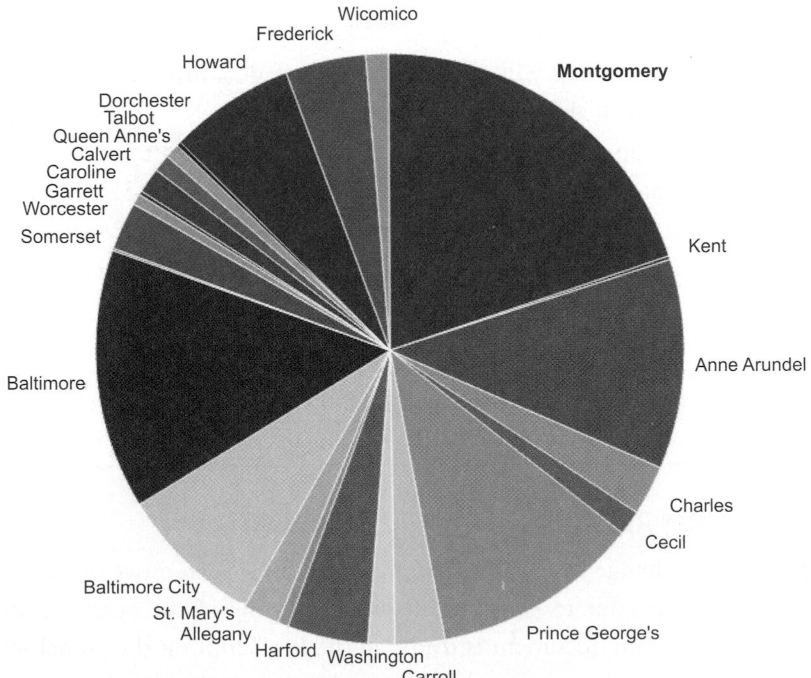

Figure 2.1 Final Pie Chart

```
var width  = 600,
    height = width,
    radius = width / 2.5,
    totals = {},
    // D3 provides a handful of color pallets
    color  = d3.scale.category20b();

// This is the circle that the pie will fill in
var arc = d3.svg.arc()
    .outerRadius(radius - 10)
    .innerRadius(0);

// D3 provides a helper function for creating the pie and slices
var pie = d3.layout.pie()
    .sort(null)
    .value(function(d) { return totals[d]; });

// Add an SVG element to the page and append a G element for the pie
var svg = d3.select("body").append("svg")
    .attr("width", width)
    .attr("height", height)
  .append("g")
    .attr("transform", "translate(" + width / 2 + "," + height / 2 +
➥")");

// Get the data and draw the slices
$.getJSON('/residential/data', function(data) {
  totals = data.totals;
  // enter is how we tell D3 to generate the SVG elements for the data
  var g = svg.selectAll(".arc")
      .data(pie(d3.keys(totals)))
    .enter().append("g")
      .attr("class", "arc")
    .on("mouseover", function(d) {
      d3.select(this).select("text").style("font-weight", "bold")
      d3.select(this).select("text").style("font-size", "1.25em")
    })
    .on("mouseout", function(d) {
      d3.select(this).select("text").style("font-weight", "normal")
      d3.select(this).select("text").style("font-size", "1em")
    })
  ;

  // color the pie slices using the color pallet
  g.append("path")
      .attr("d", arc)
      .style("fill", function(d) { return color(d.data); });

  // put the labels outside the pie (in a new arc/circle)
```

```
    var pos = d3.svg.arc().innerRadius(radius + 20).outerRadius(radius +
➥20);
    g.append("text")
        .attr("transform", function(d) { return "translate(" +
➥pos.centroid(d) + ")"; })
        .attr("dy", ".35em")
        .style("text-anchor", "middle")
        .text(function(d) { return d.data; });
  });
}
```

The G Element

You may be wondering what that G element that we added to the page along with the SVG element is all about.

The <g> element is just an SVG element that is used to group shapes together. You can transform the whole group as a single shape. In the case of the pie chart before, we added the individual pie slices to that G element. As we build more complex charts the transformations will apply more broadly, such as moving all shapes to allow room for a wider axis label.

Code Checkpoint

To see the code at this stage, go to https://github.com/DataVizToolkit/residential_sales/tree/ch02.2.

Bar Chart

The pie chart can show proportions relative to each other. A bar chart can do this as well. This time let's look at individual zip codes within one of the counties.

New Views, New Routes

To get started we can simply copy the index file and update the comment and function to be called. It's not necessarily DRY, but we are in speculative investigation mode here, exploring various chart types. The updated code for `bar_chart.html.erb` looks like this (the updated pieces are highlighted in bold):

```
<!-- A bar chart will magically appear here -->
<div id="chart"></div>

<script>
$(document).on('ready page:load', function(event) {
  // apply non-idempotent transformations to the body
  makeBar();
});
```

```
</script>
```

Next, you'll need to add these routes for the view and the data.

```
get 'residential/bar_chart'
get 'residential/bar_data', :defaults => { :format => 'json' }
```

The final view-related piece that we need to add is some style to make the bar chart look nice. Add this to `app/assets/stylesheets/residential.scss`:

```
// Bar Chart
.axis path,
.axis line {
  fill: none;
  stroke: #000;
  shape-rendering: crispEdges;
}

.bar {
  fill: steelblue;
  &:hover {
    opacity: .85;
  }
}

.x.axis path {
  fill: none;
  stroke: #000;
  shape-rendering: crispEdges;
}
```

Bar Chart Controller Actions

We need to write the ActiveRecord finder call to get the data for our bar chart, which you can see in the following. At first I had the data sorted just by zip code, which gives you a jagged bar chart. I think it's probably easier to see the bars in order of median value (the Y-axis). Feel free to play with the query and see what works for you.

```
def bar_chart; end
def bar_data
  bar_data = SalesFigure.
    select(:id, :zipcode, :median_value).
    where(:jurisdiction => 'Baltimore').
    order('median_value DESC, zipcode')
  render :json => { :bar_data => bar_data }
end
```

Bar Chart JavaScript

Now that we have the structure in place we need to create the `makeBar()` function, which you can see in Listing 2.2.

I found an example that served as a good starting point (http://bl.ocks.org/mbostock/5977197). As is typically the case, there were a handful of necessary tweaks to get the chart to work for my data:

- Our X-axis labels are longer than a single character, so the bottom margin needs to be bigger.
- Our X-axis labels need to be rotated so they don't run into each other. We need to add the rotate transform in the X-axis.
- We are not looking at percent, so we do not need the number formatter.
- We have different names in our data objects, so those selectors need to be updated.
- Rather than read a static CSV file I am making an AJAX call using jQuery.
- We use the same hover CSS to highlight a bar when you mouse over it.

The final version of the bar chart can be seen in Figure 2.2. Run `rails server` and go to http://localhost:3000/residential/bar_chart to see your bar chart.

Listing 2.2 `makeBar()` Function

```
function makeBar() {
  // From: http://bl.ocks.org/mbostock/5977197
  var margin = {top: 20, right: 20, bottom: 50, left: 50},
      width  = 960 - margin.left - margin.right,
      height = 500 - margin.top - margin.bottom;

      // data -> value
  var xValue = function(d) { return d.zipcode; },
      // value -> display
      xScale = d3.scale.ordinal().rangeRoundBands([0, width],
         .1),
      // data -> display
      xMap   = function(d) { return xScale(xValue(d)); },
      xAxis  = d3.svg.axis().scale(xScale).orient("bottom");

      // data -> value
  var yValue = function(d) { return d.median_value; },
      // value -> display
      yScale = d3.scale.linear().range([height, 0]),
      // data -> display
      yMap   = function(d) { return yScale(yValue(d)); },
      yAxis  = d3.svg.axis().scale(yScale).orient("left");
```

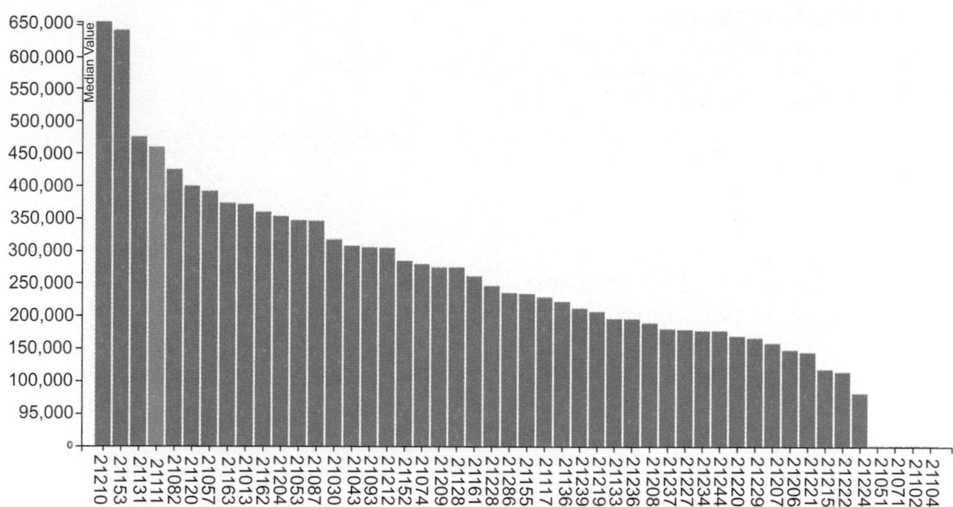

Figure 2.2 Bar Chart

```
  var svg = d3.select("#chart").append("svg")
      .attr("width", width + margin.left + margin.right)
      .attr("height", height + margin.top + margin.bottom)
    .append("g")
      .attr("transform", "translate(" + margin.left + "," + margin.top +
➥")");

  $.getJSON('/residential/bar_data', function(data) {
    data = data.bar_data;
    xScale.domain(data.map(xValue));
    yScale.domain([0, d3.max(data, yValue)]);

    svg.append("g")
        .attr("class", "x axis")
        .attr("transform", "translate(0," + height + ")")
        .call(xAxis)
      .selectAll("text")
        .attr("x", 8)
        .attr("y", -5)
        .style("text-anchor", "start")
        .attr("transform", "rotate(90)");

    svg.append("g")
        .attr("class", "y axis")
        .call(yAxis)
      .append("text")
        .attr("transform", "rotate(-90)")
```

```
          .attr("y", 6)
          .attr("dy", ".71em")
          .style("text-anchor", "end")
          .text("Median Value");

    svg.selectAll(".bar")
          .data(data)
        .enter().append("rect")
          .attr("class", "bar")
         .style("fill", "blue")
          .attr("x", xMap)
          .attr("width", xScale.rangeBand)
          .attr("y", yMap)
          .attr("height", function(d) { return height - yMap(d); });
  });
}
```

Pie, bar, and line charts are the charts you will see most commonly. I don't think the pie chart is a great representation for this data. The bar may or may not be, depending on what you're trying to show and what your audience understands about the data.

Since I'm not quite sure that we have a solid visual representation of the data, we should dig a little deeper than the pie, bar, or line graphs. Fortunately, we have more charts that we can use to help us visualize this data.

Code Checkpoint

To see the code at this stage, go to https://github.com/DataVizToolkit/residential_sales/tree/ch02.3.

Scatter Plot

Pie and bar charts are pretty standard fare. They're like the glazed and chocolate donuts in the donut store. You have to have them, and they see a lot of action. They aren't always quite what you're looking for, though. Sometimes you want a donut with sprinkles. Enter the scatter plot.

The scatter plot uses Cartesian coordinates to display values for two variables. If you don't recognize "Cartesian coordinates" by name, it refers to *x*, *y* coordinate pairs.

Scatter Plot?

A scatter plot helps you see the relationship, if any, between two continuous variables. Unlike other charts where the X-axis is treated as the independent variable (the variable that has an effect on the other variable) and the Y-axis shows the dependent variable, the scatter plot simply shows correlation. If there is also causation you would follow the dependent/independent axis convention and probably add a line of best fit such as a regression line. In a simple scatter plot, the X and Y axes have no particular meaning—either one could be used for either variable.

Scatter Plot Controller Actions

We zoomed in and looked at all the zip codes for a single jurisdiction with the bar chart. Let's take a higher-level view and look at all the zip codes. We can color-code the dots in the scatter plot, so let's use jurisdiction as our color key.

We are measuring the median value, so it goes on the Y-axis. That stays nice and consistent with the bar chart, too. The number of occurrences of each value goes on the X-axis. You could make the dot sizes indicate something, but we won't do that in this scatter plot.

The controller methods look like this:

```
def scatter_chart; end
def scatter_data
  data = SalesFigure.
    select(:id, :zipcode, :jurisdiction, :median_value, :total_sales).
    order(:jurisdiction)
  render :json => { :scatter_data => data }
end
```

Scatter Plot Views and Routes

I'm not showing the routes or the view ERB because they're consistent with the previous examples, but don't forget to add them.

We do not need a lot of new CSS for the scatter plot. You can see in the following that we have a style for a tooltip. You've seen how easy mouseover highlighting is in the pie chart. Now we are going to take the mouseover iteration a step further with a tooltip to show some additional data when you hover over one of the points.

```
// Scatter Plot
.dot {
  stroke: #000;
}

.tooltip {
  position: absolute;
  width: 200px;
  height: 28px;
  pointer-events: none;
}
```

Scatter Plot JavaScript

The code to generate our scatter plot can be seen in Listing 2.3. We did not need to stray too far from the example. Our version is a little simpler because we don't need to transform our data. One key difference is that our legend has 24 entries and is therefore too long to have in the top right corner. We break the legend into multiple columns with the help of a function nested within the transform attribute for the legend. I know I said that a legend with 24 items was too big for a chart, but the scatter plot is a lot bigger than the pie chart. The legend doesn't steal the focus in this case.

Listing 2.3 `makeScatter()` JavaScript

```
function makeScatter() {
  // From http://bl.ocks.org/weiglemc/6185069
  var margin = {top: 20, right: 20, bottom: 100, left: 150},
      width  = 960,
      height = 500 - margin.top - margin.bottom;

  /*
   * value accessor - returns the value to encode for a given data object.
   * scale - maps value to a visual display encoding, such as a pixel position.
   * map function - maps from data value to display value
   * axis - sets up axis
   */

  // setup x
      // data -> value
  var xValue = function(d) { return d.total_sales;},
      // value -> display
      xScale = d3.scale.linear().range([0, width]),
      // data -> display
      xMap   = function(d) { return xScale(xValue(d));},
      xAxis  = d3.svg.axis().scale(xScale).orient("bottom");

  // setup y
      // data -> value
  var yValue = function(d) { return d.median_value;},
      // value -> display
      yScale = d3.scale.linear().range([height, 0]),
      // data -> display
      yMap   = function(d) { return yScale(yValue(d));},
      yAxis  = d3.svg.axis().scale(yScale).orient("left");

  // setup fill color
  var cValue = function(d) { return d.jurisdiction;},
      color  = d3.scale.category20b();

  // add the graph canvas to the body of the webpage
  var svg = d3.select("#chart").append("svg")
```

```
      .attr("width", width + margin.left + margin.right)
      .attr("height", height + margin.top + margin.bottom)
    .append("g")
      .attr("transform", "translate(" + margin.left + "," + margin.top +
➥")");

  // add the tooltip area to the webpage
  var tooltip = d3.select("body").append("div")
      .attr("class", "tooltip")
      .style("opacity", 0);

  $.getJSON('/residential/scatter_data', function(data) {
    data = data.scatter_data;

    // don't want dots overlapping axis, so add in buffer to data domain
    xScale.domain([d3.min(data, xValue)-1, d3.max(data, xValue)+1]);
    yScale.domain([d3.min(data, yValue)-1, d3.max(data, yValue)+1]);

    // x-axis
    svg.append("g")
        .attr("class", "x axis")
        .attr("transform", "translate(0," + height + ")")
        .call(xAxis)
      .append("text")
        .attr("class", "label")
        .attr("x", width)
        .attr("y", -6)
        .style("text-anchor", "end")
        .text("Total Sales");

    // y-axis
    svg.append("g")
        .attr("class", "y axis")
        .call(yAxis)
      .append("text")
        .attr("class", "label")
        .attr("transform", "rotate(-90)")
        .attr("y", 6)
        .attr("dy", ".71em")
        .style("text-anchor", "end")
        .text("Median Value");

    // draw dots
    svg.selectAll(".dot")
        .data(data)
      .enter().append("circle")
        .attr("class", "dot")
        .attr("r", 3.5)
        .attr("cx", xMap)
        .attr("cy", yMap)
```

```
        .style("fill", function(d) { return color(cValue(d));})
        .on("mouseover", function(d) {
            tooltip.transition()
                 .duration(200)
                 .style("opacity", .9);
            tooltip.html(d.zipcode + "<br/> (" + xValue(d)
            + ", $" + yValue(d) + ")")
                 .style("left", (d3.event.pageX + 5) + "px")
                 .style("top", (d3.event.pageY - 28) + "px");
        })
        .on("mouseout", function(d) {
            tooltip.transition()
                 .duration(500)
                 .style("opacity", 0);
        });

    // draw legend
    var legend = svg.selectAll(".legend")
        .data(color.domain())
      .enter().append("g")
        .attr("class", "legend")
        .attr("transform", function(d, i) {
          numCols = 8;
          xOff = (i % numCols) * 120 + 50;
          yOff = Math.floor(i / numCols) * 20
          return "translate(" + xOff + "," + yOff + ")"
        });

    // draw legend colored rectangles
    legend.append("rect")
        .attr("x", margin.left - 100)
        .attr("y", height + margin.top)
        .attr("width", 18)
        .attr("height", 18)
        .style("fill", color);

    // draw legend text
    legend.append("text")
        .attr("x", margin.left - 100)
        .attr("y", height + 29)
        .attr("dy", ".35em")
        .style("text-anchor", "end")
        .text(function(d) { return d; })
  });
}
```

You can see the scatter plot with a tooltip visible in Figure 2.3.

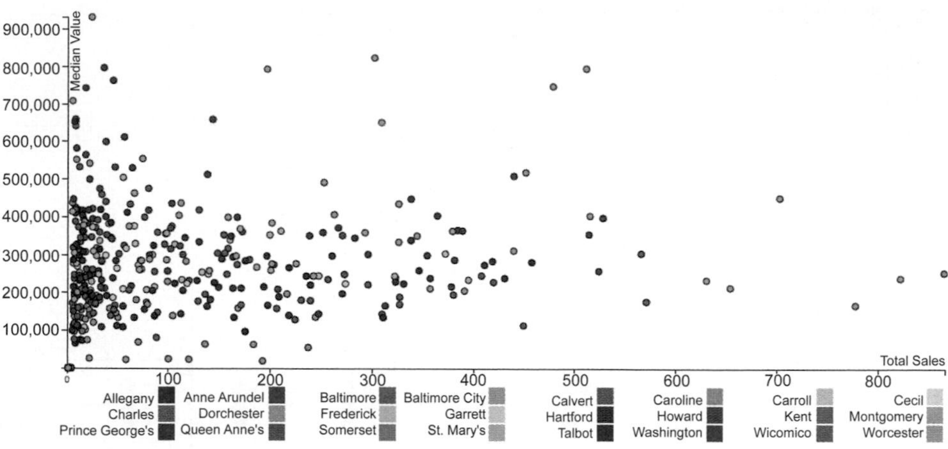

Figure 2.3 Scatter Plot

Code Checkpoint

To see the code at this stage, go to https://github.com/DataVizToolkit/residential_sales/tree/ch02.4.

Scatter Plot Revisited

We can definitely see a cluster of points where the median value is between $100,000 and $500,000. It's sort of a jumbled mess, though. What would be really nice is if we could isolate each jurisdiction.

Fortunately, with a couple of minor tweaks we can! We can attach `mouseover` and `mouseout` events to the elements in the legend to show or hide points based on which jurisdiction they belong to. So we need to add a CSS selector to each point and then add the events.

We change the CSS class that we assign to the dots to include `dot` and also the jurisdiction's name. This is data that we have access to in both this section of the chart generation as well as in the legend. Note the gnarly regular expression in the `replace()`. That's because we need to trim out spaces, apostrophes, and periods in the names in order to make them valid CSS selectors that we can grab with jQuery.

```
.attr("class", function(d) {
  return "dot " + cValue(d).replace(/\W+/g, "");
})
```

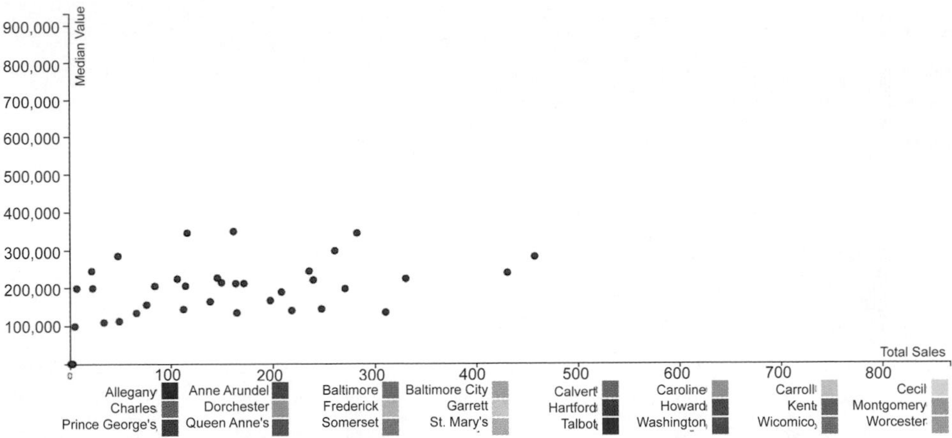

Figure 2.4 Scatter Plot for a Single Jurisdiction

Next, we'll add the mouse events to the color squares (rectangles) in the legend. When you hover over one, all the dots will be hidden, and then just the dots that correspond to that jurisdiction will reappear. When you mouse out all the dots will reappear.

```
.style("fill", color)
.on("mouseover", function(d, i) {
  name = d.replace(/\W+/g, "")
  $('.dot').hide();
  $('.' + name).show();
})
.on("mouseout", function(d, i) {
  $('.dot').show(1);
});
```

Great! Now we have a scatter plot that we can use to start making sense of the data for the various jurisdictions. You can see the scatter plots with just Prince George's jurisdiction visible in Figure 2.4.

Code Checkpoint

To see the code at this stage, go to https://github.com/DataVizToolkit/residential_sales/tree/ch02.5.

Box Plot

Continuing with the donut shop analogy, donuts are great but sometimes you want a cinnamon roll. We saw a fair amount of variance in the median prices. A box plot is a way to look at how tight or varied your data is. You can also see the outliers more clearly. As we saw with the scatter plot, there is a lot of variance in the data. It also looks like maybe we have some junk data.

According to Wikipedia, "The box plot (a.k.a. box and whisker diagram) is a standardized way of displaying the distribution of data based on the five number summary: minimum, first quartile, median, third quartile, and maximum."

That's a lot of fancy statistics jargon, but it's not so scary.

Quartiles

Quartiles simply divide a set of numbers into quarters. Think of the set of scores as being sorted in order (e.g., 1, 1, 1, 2, 2, 3, 3, 3, 3, 4, 5, 5). One fourth of the scores will fall into the first quarter of that ordered set, one fourth will fall into the second quarter, and so forth (see Figure 2.1 for an example). The median sets the second quartile (Q2) because it is the middle score. The first quartile (Q1) is the midpoint between the lowest number and the median, and the third quartile (Q3) is the midpoint between the median and the highest number. Those 3 points divide the set or ordered numbers into 4 pieces. If you divided the data into 5 pieces they would be quintiles, and so on. Just as with the median, if the number of scores in a quartile is even it could be that you will have two scores of different values at the midpoint. In that case you add them together and take the average to find the quartile. For a clear explanation of quartiles go to https://www.mathsisfun.com/data/quartiles.html.

Boxes, Whiskers, Circles, What?!

When you look at a box plot, also known as a box-and-whisker diagram, you see a rectangle with a line in the middle of it. That middle line is the median, and the rectangle shows the space from Q1 to Q2 and Q2 to Q3. The whiskers (lines) show the variability outside the lower and upper quartiles. Anything outside that is an outlier and shown as a dot.

Box Plot Data and Views

I'm going to use the same data for the box plot that we used for the scatter plot, so the data route will remain `residential/scatter_data`. We need to add a new ERB file (`app/views/residential/boxplot.html.erb`) and its corresponding controller method:

```
def boxplot; end
```

The view will call `makeBoxplot()`. We also need a new route for the box plot view:

```
get 'residential/boxplot'
```

The CSS can be seen here:

```
// Boxplot
.box {
  font: 10px sans-serif;
}

.box line,
.box rect,
.box circle {
  fill: steelblue;
  stroke: #000;
  stroke-width: 1px;
}

.box .center {
  stroke-dasharray: 3,3;
}

.box .outlier {
  fill: none;
  stroke: #000;
}
```

Box Plot JavaScript

The first thing I always do when I need to make a chart is find prior art to see some examples. It looks like we need to include some additional code to tell D3 how to make a box plot. There is a file `box.js` that the examples all have, and is pretty similar. You can grab the file from https://raw.githubusercontent.com/DataVizToolkit/residential_sales/master/vendor/assets/javascripts/box.js and save it to `vendor/assets/javascripts`. Then, in application.js, require the file (`//= require box`). Alternatively, you can include the script in the application layout where the others are listed.

We also need to calculate interquartile range, which is a fancy way of saying "the space in the middle" or Q3 - Q1 (again, an excellent explanation can be found at https://www.mathsisfun.com/data/quartiles.html). Here is the `iqr` function.

```
// Returns a function to compute the interquartile range.
function iqr(k) {
  return function(d, i) {
    var q1 = d.quartiles[0],
        q3 = d.quartiles[2],
        iqr = (q3 - q1) * k,
        i = -1,
        j = d.length;
    while (d[++i] < q1 - iqr);
```

```
    while (d[--j] > q3 + iqr);
    return [i, j];
  };
}
```

And with that we are now ready to draw some boxes, whiskers, and circles. Listing 2.4 handles that for us.

We haven't had to transform the data that we've pulled from the database yet. To calculate the quartiles, we need the data in a particular format, though. My data is different from the examples, but I like the way they draw the chart. So I just rearrange my data into the format that they want. I like using `map-reduce` to iterate over and transform data.

Listing 2.4 **`makeBoxplot`** **Function**

```
function makeBoxplot() {
  // From: http://bl.ocks.org/mbostock/4061502
  // From: http://bl.ocks.org/jensgrubert/7789216
  var margin = {top: 30, right: 50, bottom: 95, left: 50},
      width  = 900 - margin.left - margin.right;
      height = 450 - margin.top - margin.bottom,
      min    = Infinity,
      max    = -Infinity,
      labels = false; // show the text labels beside individual boxplots?

  $.getJSON('/residential/scatter_data', function(d) {
    // Create arrays of median values for each jurisdiction
    data = d.scatter_data.reduce(function(accum, obj) {
      indices = accum.map(function(arr) { return arr[0]; });
      idx = indices.indexOf(obj.jurisdiction);
      value = +obj.median_value;
      if (idx > -1) {
        accum[idx][1].push(value);
      } else {
        accum.push([obj.jurisdiction, [value]]);
      }
      if (value > max) { max = value; }
      if (value < min) { min = value; }
      return accum;
    }, []);

    var chart = d3.box()
      .whiskers(iqr(1.5))
      .height(height)
      .domain([min, max])
      .showLabels(labels);

    var svg = d3.select("#chart").append("svg")
```

```
      .attr("width", width + margin.left + margin.right)
      .attr("height", height + margin.top + margin.bottom)
      .attr("class", "box")
      .append("g")
      .attr("transform", "translate(" + margin.left + "," + margin.top +
➥")");

    // the x-axis
    var x = d3.scale.ordinal()
      .domain( data.map(function(d) { return d[0] } ) )
      .rangeRoundBands([0 , width], 0.7, 0.3);

    var xAxis = d3.svg.axis()
      .scale(x)
      .orient("bottom");

    // the y-axis
    var y = d3.scale.linear()
      .domain([min, max])
      .range([height + margin.top, 0 + margin.top]);

    var yAxis = d3.svg.axis()
      .scale(y)
      .orient("left");

    // draw the boxplots
    svg.selectAll(".box")
        .data(data)
      .enter().append("g")
      .attr("transform", function(d) { return "translate(" +  x(d[0])  +
➥"," + margin.top + ")"; } )
        .call(chart.width(x.rangeBand()));

    // add a title
    svg.append("text")
       .attr("x", (width / 2))
       .attr("y", 0 + (margin.top / 2))
       .attr("text-anchor", "middle")
       .style("font-size", "18px")
       //.style("text-decoration", "underline")
       .text("Median Home Sale Value By Jurisdiction");

    // draw y axis
    svg.append("g")
       .attr("class", "y axis")
       .call(yAxis);

    // draw x axis
    svg.append("g")
```

```
        .attr("class", "x axis")
        .attr("transform", "translate(0," + (height  + margin.top) + ")")
        .call(xAxis)
      .selectAll("text")
        .attr("x", -5)
        .attr("y", 5)
        .style("text-anchor", "end")
        .attr("transform", "rotate(-45)");
  });
}
```

The finished, transformed, data is an array of arrays like the following example:

```
 [
  ["Jurisdiction1", [100, 200, 300]],
  ["Jurisdiction2", [100, 200, 300]],
  ["Jurisdiction3", [100, 200, 300]],
]
```

Aside from transforming the data we didn't have to diverge too far from the examples. The `box.js` code will sort the arrays of values, so we don't need to worry about that.

Now we can clearly see in Figure 2.5 that there is a value that hugs the X axis. This is probably some sort of default or placeholder data that we don't really want or need. We can add a filter to the data easily, like the bolded line in the following listing.

```
def scatter_data
  data = SalesFigure.
    select(:id, :zipcode, :jurisdiction, :median_value, :total_sales).
    where('median_value > 1000').
    order(:jurisdiction)
  render :json => { :scatter_data => data }
end
```

Figure 2.6 shows the updated box plot with some fairly different lower quartiles. Go back and see how that change affected the scatter plot too.

Code Checkpoint

To see the code at this stage, go to https://github.com/DataVizToolkit/residential_sales/tree/ch02.6.

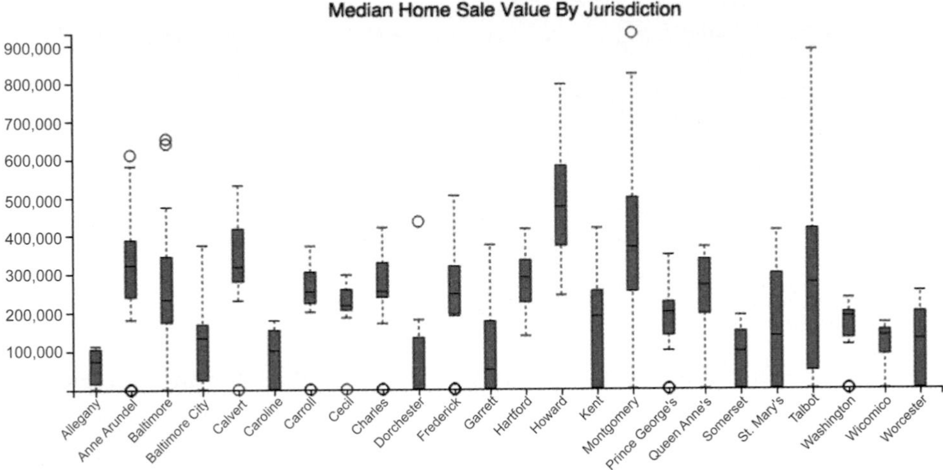

Figure 2.5 Box Plot

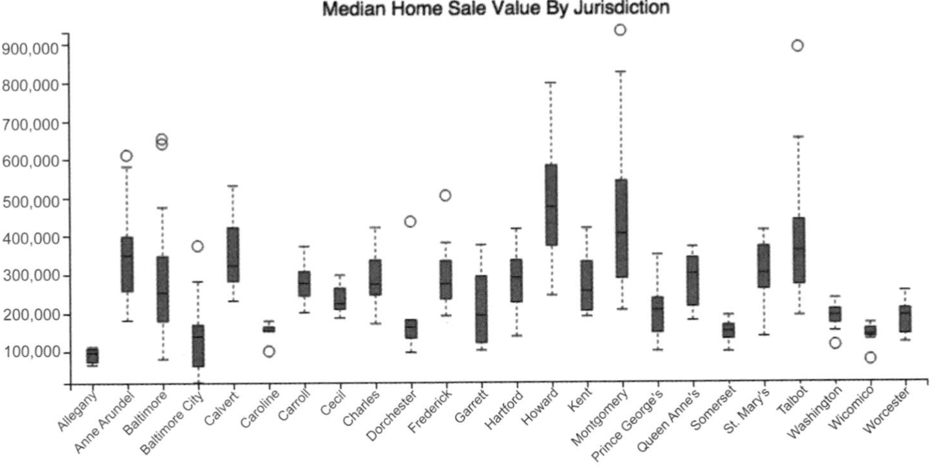

Figure 2.6 Updated Box Plot without Default Values

Summary

In this chapter we revisited the pie chart from Chapter 1, "D3 and Rails," to make it more legible and add interactivity. We also looked at three new types of charts: bar, scatter, and box. We learned some fun statistics terms, and we were able to look at our data and see how the various zip codes and jurisdictions compare to each other. The data transformation that we did to line up the data and then calculate the interquartile ranges can also be done in the database. We will get to that a little later in this book.

Chapter 3
Working with Time Series Data

In the last chapter, we looked at four different types of graphs: pie, bar, scatter plot, and box plot. In this chapter we slow down a little and focus on building up a multi-line graph using historic weather data. The data is available from the Global Historical Climatology Network (GHCN) via NOAA (https://www.ncdc.noaa.gov/data-access/land-based-station-data/land-based-datasetsglobal-historical-climatology-network-ghcn).

The GHCN provides a rich set of data. There are weather stations around the world and readings going back as far as 1763. I chose a relatively small data file from 1836 for this chapter. In that year there were five stations reporting temperature.

Let's see what that data looks like!

Historic Daily Weather Data

There are two files that you need to download. Most of the links from the NOAA site seem to link to their FTP site, but the files are actually available via FTP or HTTP. HTTP is easier to script.

Download these files:

- http://www1.ncdc.noaa.gov/pub/data/ghcn/daily/by_year/1836.csv.gz
- http://www1.ncdc.noaa.gov/pub/data/ghcn/daily/ghcnd-stations.txt

The first file has all the daily readings from the year 1836. There are several different measurements for each day, including minimum observed temperature and maximum observed temperature. Temperature is what we will be looking at with this graph.

The second file is the list of all the weather stations. It includes the weather station identifier we need to join to the readings, as well as the station's coordinates. By joining the station coordinates with the readings, we know the locations where each reading was recorded. We will do more with the geographic aspect a little later in this book in Chapter 10, "Making Maps with Leaflet and Rails."

NOAA also provides a `README` with an explanation of the data files that they offer. You can find that at http://www1.ncdc.noaa.gov/pub/data/ghcn/daily/by_year/readme.txt.

Weather Rails App

Now that we have a handle on the data files, it's time to create the Rails app and import some data. I called my app `weather`:

```
rails new weather --database=postgresql
```

Code Checkpoint

To see the code at this stage, go to https://github.com/DataVizToolkit/weather/tree/ch03.1.

Weather Readings Model

The documentation that I referred to is essentially a launching point to more documentation. The layout of the daily files is in a rich text format file, which is also available on the server. This data set was a little hard to get a handle on because of all the different places you have to look for related data and explanations of the data.

No worry, though. I've gone through and mapped it all out. The migration for the weather readings model is shown in the following:

```
rails g model weather_reading station reading_date:date \
  reading_type reading_value:integer measurement_flag quality_flag \
  source_flag observation_time:integer
```

Don't forget to create your database (`bundle exec rake db:create`) and run the migration (`bundle exec rake db:migrate`).

Weather Readings Import

Put the file we downloaded in `db/data_files`. The rake task to import the data is shown in Listing 3.1. We can create the task's file using the Rails generator (`rails g task seed`), or by simply creating the file (`lib/tasks/seed.rake`). The name is not critical to its function. It should just be clear enough that you know what it does when you see it.

Listing 3.1 Weather Readings Import

```
require 'csv'
namespace :db do
  namespace :seed do
    desc "Import NOAA weather CSV"
    task :import_noaa_weather => :environment do

      filename = File.join(Rails.root, 'db', 'data_files', '1836.csv')
      CSV.foreach(filename, :headers => false) do |row|
        puts $. if $. % 10000 == 0
        date_parts = row[1].match(/(\d{4})(\d{2})(\d{2})/)
        date = Date.civil(date_parts[1].to_i, date_parts[2].to_i,
➥date_parts[3].to_i)
        data = {
          :station            => row[0],
          :reading_date       => date,
          :reading_type       => row[2],
          :reading_value      => Integer(row[3]),
          :measurement_flag => row[4],
          :quality_flag       => row[5],
          :source_flag        => row[6],
          :observation_time => row[7]
        }
        WeatherReading.create(data)
      end
    end
  end
end
```

That weird row with the dollar signs takes advantage of a strange holdover from Ruby's Perl heritage. The dollar dot variable (`$.`) tells you the last line number read from a file.

We want to run the rake task in the context of the Rails app's Gemfile. Bundler can help us with that. Execute the rake task by running

```
bundle exec rake db:seed:import_noaa_weather
```

After you run the rake task, remember to take a look at the data to make sure it makes sense.

Weather Stations Model

We have an identifier for the weather station in each of the readings. Let's go ahead and import the data to tell us what and where the weather stations are. The migration for the weather stations model follows.

```
rails g model weather_station station_id:index \
  latitude:float longitude:float elevation:float state name \
  gsn_flag hcn_flag wmo_id
```

You may notice that we took advantage of the ability to define an index in the migration. The station ID is a foreign key that we will refer to from the weather readings. It's generally a good idea to put an index on any field that would commonly be used in a JOIN clause, such as foreign keys. We will talk more about foreign keys in Chapter 6, "The Chord Diagram."

Weather Stations Import

There are a little over 96,000 weather stations listed in our file! Needless to say, this file is going to take a little longer to import. The rake task for that is shown in Listing 3.2, and I put it in the same file with the other import task.

To execute this rake task we run:

```
bundle exec rake db:seed:import_noaa_stations
```

Listing 3.2 Weather Stations Import

```
desc "Import NOAA weather station data"
task :import_noaa_stations => :environment do
  def safe_string(str)
    str.strip!
    str.empty? ? nil : str
  end

  filename = File.join(Rails.root, 'db', 'data_files', 'ghcnd-
➥stations.txt')
  File.open(filename, "r") do |f|
    f.each_with_index do |line, index|
      puts index if index > 0 && index % 10000 == 0
      data = {
        :station_id => line[0..10],
        :latitude   => safe_string(line[11..19]),
        :longitude  => safe_string(line[20..29]),
        :elevation  => safe_string(line[30..36]),
        :state      => safe_string(line[38..39]),
        :name       => safe_string(line[41..70]),
        :gsn_flag   => safe_string(line[72..74]),
```

```
        :hcn_flag     => safe_string(line[76..78]),
        :wmo_id       => safe_string(line[80..84])
      }
      WeatherStation.create(data)
    end
  end
end
```

We aren't using the dollar dot variable here. Instead we are using `Enumerable#each_with_index` to get the line number as we read lines from the file.

Code Checkpoint

To see the code at this stage, go to https://github.com/DataVizToolkit/weather/tree/ch03.2.

Simple Line Graph

I've mentioned before that I like to start simple and build on top of that foundation. I have a graph in mind that displays the daily minimum and maximum temperatures, but for starters I want to just get the most basic graph possible in place.

At first I thought about graphing all the maximum temperatures for all the weather stations. That doesn't really scale, though. Even with five weather stations it was a mess. They all generally followed the same pattern, too. We can do more interesting visualizations with the data for a single weather station that will be more communicative and more visually appealing. It may seem like overkill to have loaded all 96,000 stations, but we will come back and do more in Chapter 5, "Window Functions, Subqueries, and Common Table Expression."

Weather Controller

Wouldn't it be great if you could make something to control the weather? I can't help with that, but I can tell you that it's time to create the `weather_controller.rb` file, like so:

```
rails g controller weather index --no-helper
```

I pass in the switch to tell the generator to not create any helper files. The bulk of what we are going to do is JavaScript.

Fetch the Data

The generator that we ran created the route and the `index.html.erb` file that we need. We need to manually add a route for the data call. That looks like this:

```
get 'weather/data', :defaults => { :format => 'json' }
```

With that in place we are ready to fetch the data in the controller, which you can see in Listing 3.3. You'll note that this find is a little more complex. We are doing a join to pull in the weather station data. The benefit to doing a join is that we pull in the related data in the initial query rather than having to ask for it later, one record at a time. See Appendix C, "SQL Join Overview," for more on SQL joins.

Listing 3.3 Weather Data Controller with Data Fetch

```
class WeatherController < ApplicationController
  def index; end
  def data
    readings = WeatherReading.
      joins(:weather_station).
      where(:reading_type => "TMAX").
      where("weather_stations.name = 'MILAN'").
      order("reading_type, reading_date").
      select("weather_readings.id, reading_date, reading_type,
➥reading_value, source_flag, latitude, longitude, elevation, name")
    render :json => { :readings => readings }
  end
end
```

In order for Rails to know how to execute the join we need to tell the models how they are related. A `WeatherReading` has one `WeatherStation`. That association can be expressed by adding this line to the `WeatherReading` model:

```
has_one :weather_station, :foreign_key => 'station_id', :primary_key => 'station'
```

The `has_one` association is more verbose than you may be accustomed to seeing. The tables do not follow the Rails convention for foreign keys, so we need to specify the fields.

We add this line to the `WeatherStation` model to express the inverse relationship and allow a `WeatherReading` object to know which `WeatherStation` it belongs to:

```
belongs_to :weather_reading
```

The SQL that is generated when we run the code looks like this:

```
SELECT wr.id, wr.station, wr.reading_type, wr.reading_value,
➥wr.source_flag,
```

```
  ws.latitude, ws.longitude, ws.elevation, ws.name
FROM weather_readings wr
JOIN weather_stations ws on station = ws.station_id
WHERE reading_type = 'TMAX'
ORDER BY reading_type, reading_date
```

The View Files

We need to update the `index.html.erb` file for the view, and it will look a lot like the other views that we've done.

```
<script>
$(document).on('ready page:load', function(event) {
  makeLineChart();
});
</script>
```

The CSS that we will use for the line graph(s) follows. Include it in `weather.scss`.

```
body {
  font: 10px sans-serif;
}

.axis path,
.axis line {
  fill: none;
  stroke: #000;
  shape-rendering: crispEdges;
}

.line {
  fill: none;
  stroke: steelblue;
  stroke-width: 1.5px;
}
```

We also need to include the D3 library in our application's layout file (`app/views/layouts/application.html.erb`). Add this line before the application's JavaScript is included:

```
<%= javascript_include_tag
➥"https://cdnjs.cloudflare.com/ajax/libs/d3/3.5.17/d3.min.js" %>
```

Draw the Line Graph

The JavaScript to draw the simple line graph is nearly 100 lines (see Listing 3.4). That sets us up nicely for a series of small tweaks that we will make to get to the final graph. I have included a lot of comments to explain what each section of the code does.

The data transformation is similar to the `reduce` that we did for the scatter plot in Chapter 2, "Transforming Data with ActiveRecord and D3." We are creating an array of objects for each reading type. In this first graph, there is only one reading type (TMAX). Each reading type object includes an array of readings that are ordered by date thanks to the query.

Start the Rails server (`rails server`) and navigate your browser to http://localhost:3000/weather/index, and you should see something that looks like Figure 3.1.

Listing 3.4 `makeLineChart()` JavaScript

```
function makeLineChart() {
  // based on http://bl.ocks.org/mbostock/3884955
  var margin = {top: 20, right: 80, bottom: 30, left: 50},
      width  = 960 - margin.left - margin.right,
      height = 500 - margin.top - margin.bottom;

  // define accessors for the x and y values
  var x      = d3.time.scale().range([0, width]),
      y      = d3.scale.linear().range([height, 0]);

  // setup the x and y axes
  var xAxis = d3.svg.axis().scale(x).orient("bottom"),
      yAxis = d3.svg.axis().scale(y).orient("left");

  // helper functions for date formatting and color(s) for the line(s)
  var parseDate  = d3.time.format("%Y-%m-%d").parse,
      color      = d3.scale.category10();

  // define the line(s) as a series of points from the data
  var line = d3.svg.line()
      .x(function(d) { return x(d.reading_date); })
      .y(function(d) { return y(d.reading_value); });

  // add the chart SVG to the body
  var svg = d3.select("body").append("svg")
      .attr("width", width + margin.left + margin.right)
      .attr("height", height + margin.top + margin.bottom)
    .append("g")
      .attr("transform", "translate(" + margin.left + "," + margin.top +
➥")");
```

```
// fetch and process the data
$.getJSON('/weather/data', function(data) {
  data = data.readings;

  // NOTE: temperature in tenths of degrees C
  var readingTypes = function(reading) { return reading.reading_type };
  var readings = data.reduce(function(readings, reading) {
    reading.reading_date = parseDate(reading.reading_date);
    reading.reading_value = reading.reading_value*0.1 * 9/5 + 32;
    indices = readings.map(readingTypes);
    idx = indices.indexOf(reading.reading_type);
    if (idx > -1) {
      readings[idx].values.push(reading)
    } else {
      readings.push({
        reading_type: reading.reading_type,
        values: [reading]
      });
    }
    return readings;
  }, []);
  color.domain(readings.map(readingTypes));

  // set the upper and lower range for the axes
  x.domain(d3.extent(data, function(d) { return d.reading_date; }));
  y.domain(d3.extent(data, function(d) { return d.reading_value; }));

  // put the x axis into the graph
  svg.append("g")
      .attr("class", "x axis")
      .attr("transform", "translate(0," + height + ")")
      .call(xAxis);

  // put the y axis into the graph
  svg.append("g")
      .attr("class", "y axis")
      .call(yAxis)
    .append("text")
      .attr("transform", "rotate(-90)")
      .attr("y", 6)
      .attr("dy", ".71em")
      .style("text-anchor", "end")
      .text("Temperature (°F)");

  // create the SVG element for the line(s) and feed the data to it
  var station = svg.selectAll(".station")
      .data(readings)
```

```
      .enter().append("g")
        .attr("class", "station");

    // generate the points and line(s) based on the data
    station.append("path")
        .attr("class", "line")
        .attr("d", function(d) { return line(d.values); })
        .style("stroke", function(d) { return color(d.reading_type); });

    // append a label at the end of the line for the reading type
    station.append("text")
        .datum(function(d) { return {reading_type: d.reading_type, value:
➥d.values[d.values.length - 1]}; })
        .attr("transform", function(d) { return "translate(" +
➥x(d.value.reading_date) + "," + y(d.value.reading_value) + ")"; })
        .attr("x", 3)
        .attr("dy", ".35em")
        .text(function(d) { return d.reading_type; });
  });
}
```

Code Checkpoint

To see the code at this stage, go to https://github.com/DataVizToolkit/weather/tree/ch03.3.

Tweak 1: Simple Multiline Graph

With just two small updates, one in the JavaScript and one in the controller, we can display both the maximum and minimum temperatures for each day.

First, we change the `find` method in the controller to look for `"TMAX" OR "TMIN"`. ActiveRecord is pretty clever about this. You can pass an array into a `where` method, and it'll convert the SQL to an "IN" query instead of looking for where the value equals just the one thing. Update the first `where` line in the controller to read:

```
where(:reading_type => ["TMAX", "TMIN"]).
```

If you refresh the page at this point you'll see two lines, and each line will be labeled at the end with what it represents. That's fine, but we don't really want the `category10` color palette. We can represent the maximum and minimum temperature lines with colors that are more meaningful. Red is typically "hotter" and blue is typically "colder," so let's use that visual cue to our advantage.

Change the line in `makeLineChart()` where we define the `color` variable to the following:

Figure 3.1 Simple Line Graph for Maximum Temperatures

```
color        = d3.scale.ordinal()
                 .domain(["TMAX", "TMIN"])
                 .range(["red", "blue"]);
```

There is a lot happening in that tweak to the `color` variable. The `category10` color scheme is an **ordinal** scheme. Ordinal means that it relates to the item's position in a series. TMAX is the first item in the series. We use ordinal scales where we care about the order of things such as rank.

Another kind of scale that we use in D3 is called **quantitative**. We use the quantitative scale for things that fall along a continuum, such as weight or length.

Refresh the page now and you should see Figure 3.2.

Code Checkpoint

To see the code at this stage, go to https://github.com/DataVizToolkit/weather/tree/ch03.4.

Tweak 2: Add Circle to Highlight the Maximum Temperature

The lines look good, but don't do much. Let's add some `mouseover` interactivity to the graph. To do that we start by simply putting a circle on the maximum temperature line at the point on the x-axis where the mouse is. The article that I drew inspiration from to make the next sequence of changes can be found at http://www.d3noob.org/2014/07/my-favourite-tooltip-method-for-line.html.

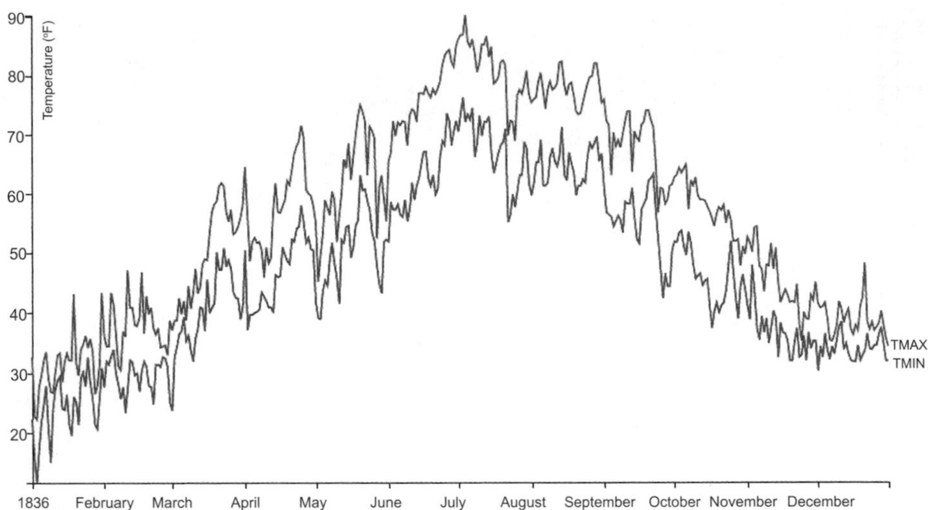

Figure 3.2 Maximum and Minimum Temperatures Graphed

There are two updates that we need to make in the JavaScript function to make this happen. We add some variables that you can put immediately before the `$.getJSON` block:

```
// add focus circles
var bisectDate = d3.bisector(function(d) { return d.reading_date;
➥}).left,
    focusMax = svg.append("g").style("display", "none");
```

The `focusMax` variable creates the SVG element that we will use for the circle. The `bisectDate` function is a way for us to get to the `reading_date` based on where the mouse is. You can read more about bisecting arrays with D3 in the documentation at https://github.com/mbostock/d3/wiki/Arrays.

With those variables in place, we are ready to trap the mouse events and draw the circle. Put this code at the end of the `$.getJSON` function:

Listing 3.5 Add Focus Circle to the Maximum Temperature Line

```
// append the circle at the intersection
focusMax.append("circle")
    .attr("class", "y")
    .style("fill", "none")
    .style("stroke", "black")
    .attr("r", 4);

// append a rectangle to capture mouse
```

```
svg.append("rect")
    .attr("width", width)
    .attr("height", height)
    .style("fill", "none")
    .style("pointer-events", "all")
    .on("mouseover", function() {
      focusMax.style("display", null);
    })
    .on("mouseout", function() {
      focusMax.style("display", "none");
    })
    .on("mousemove", mousemove);

function mousemove() {
  var x0     = x.invert(d3.mouse(this)[0]),
      iMax   = bisectDate(readings[0].values, x0, 1),
      d0Max = readings[0].values[iMax - 1],
      d1Max = readings[0].values[iMax],
      dMax   = x0 - d0Max.reading_date > d1Max.reading_date - x0 ? d1Max:
➥d0Max;

  focusMax.select("circle.y")
      .attr("transform",
            "translate(" + x(dMax.reading_date) + "," +
                          y(dMax.reading_value) + ")");
}
```

Refresh the page, and you should be able to move the mouse around the graph and see a circle track along the red line (see Figure 3.3).

Code Checkpoint

To see the code at this stage, go to https://github.com/DataVizToolkit/weather/tree/ch03.5.

Tweak 3: Add Circle to Highlight the Minimum Temperature

Now that we have highlighted the maximum temperature we should also highlight the minimum temperature. We can piggyback on what we did in the previous step to add a second circle. First we define another SVG element that we call `focusMin`. Put this immediately before the `focusMax` variable is defined:

```
focusMin = svg.append("g").style("display", "none"),
```

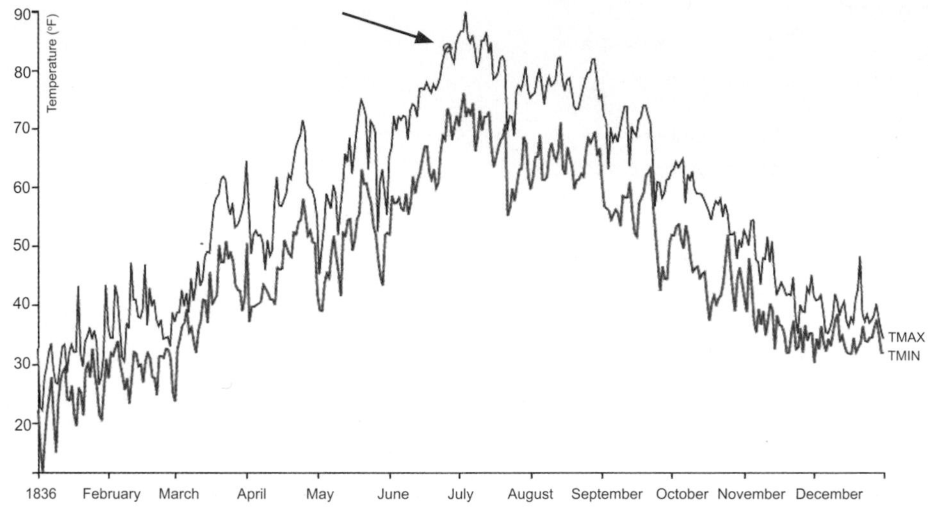

Figure 3.3 Maximum Temperature Focus Circle

Then we add that circle to the minimum temperature line like we did for the maximum temperature before. Put this with its `focusMax` counterpart:

```
focusMin.append("circle")
    .attr("class", "y")
    .style("fill", "none")
    .style("stroke", "black")
    .attr("r", 4);
```

Add `mouseover` and `mouseout` events for `focusMin` that mirror the `focusMax` events. For example, here is one:

```
focusMin.style("display", null);
```

We need to define more variables in the `mousemove()` function to help draw the `focusMin` circle. We can put these immediately after the `x0` variable is defined:

```
iMin  = bisectDate(readings[1].values, x0, 1),
d0Min = readings[1].values[iMin - 1],
d1Min = readings[1].values[iMin],
dMin  = x0 - d0Min.reading_date > d1Min.reading_date - x0 ? d1Min : d0Min;
```

Finally, we can place the circle on the line where it needs to be for the mouseover:

```
focusMin.select("circle.y")
    .attr("transform",
```

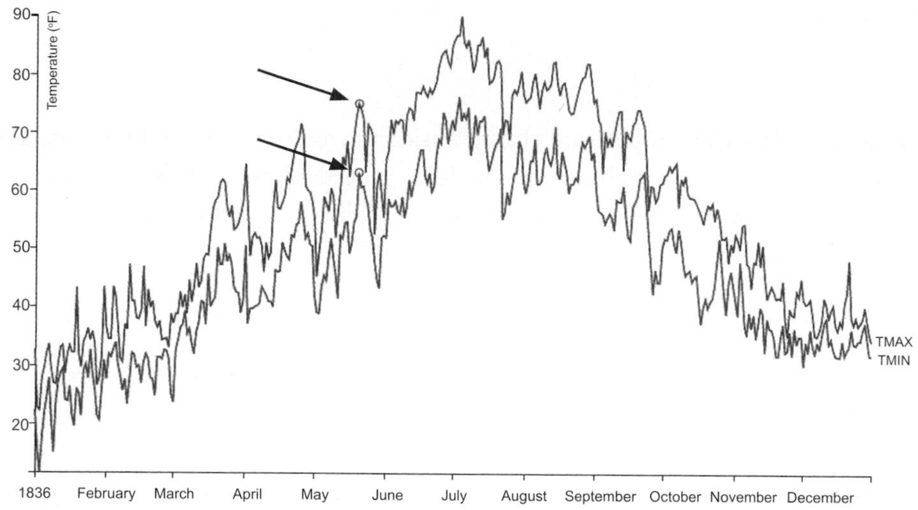

Figure 3.4 Focus Circles on Both Lines

```
        "translate(" + x(dMin.reading_date) + "," +
                       y(dMin.reading_value) + ")");
```

Code Checkpoint

To see the code at this stage, go to https://github.com/DataVizToolkit/weather/tree/ch03.6.

Tweak 4: Add Text to Display the Temperature Change

We have the two foci that highlight the maximum and minimum temperatures for the day. However, we have to eyeball the graph to get a sense of the difference between the temperatures for any given day. Let's calculate and display the actual value.

First, we need to append a text label to the maximum temperature circle. We have to define `y1` and `y2` to designate how wide the text label will be. We can put these lines after the `focusMax.append` that we already have:

```
// append a text label to the max temp line for the daily temp change
focusMax.append("text")
    .attr("class", "y1")
    .style("stroke", "white")
    .style("stroke-width", "3.5px")
    .style("opacity", 0.8)
    .attr("dx", 8)
    .attr("dy", "-.3em");
focusMax.append("text")
```

```
    .attr("class", "y2")
    .attr("dx", 8)
    .attr("dy", "-.3em");
```

Next we calculate the temperature change inside the `mousemove()` function. We use the `dMax` and `dMin` variables in this code, so it needs to go after the definition of those variables. Change the semicolon at the end of the `dMax` definition to a comma and add this line:

```
delta = (dMax.reading_value - dMin.reading_value).toFixed(1);
```

Finally, we fill in the text for the label. Put this at the end of the `mousemove()` function:

```
focusMax.select("text.y1")
    .text(delta + '°')
    .attr("transform",
          "translate(" + x(dMax.reading_date) + "," +
                         y(dMax.reading_value) + ")");
focusMax.select("text.y2")
    .text(delta + '°')
    .attr("transform",
          "translate(" + x(dMax.reading_date) + "," +
                         y(dMax.reading_value) + ")");
```

Refresh the page and you should see Figure 3.5.

Code Checkpoint

To see the code at this stage, go to https://github.com/DataVizToolkit/weather/tree/ch03.7.

Tweak 5: Add a Line Between the Focus Circles

The label with the temperature change is nice, but I think that we can make one more improvement to help show how big or small the daily temperature change is. We can draw a vertical line between the two focal points.

First, we append one more element to the `focusMax` line:

```
// append the line between the max and min temperature circles
focusMax.append("line")
    .attr("class", "x")
    .style("stroke", "black")
    .style("stroke-dasharray", "3,3")
    .style("opacity", 0.5)
    .attr("y1", 0)
```

```
    .attr("y2", height);
```

Then we make one more update inside the `mousemove()` function:

```
focusMax.select(".x")
        .attr("transform",
              "translate(" + x(dMax.reading_date) + "," +
                             y(dMax.reading_value) + ")")
                   .attr("y2", y(dMin.reading_value) -
➥y(dMax.reading_value));
```

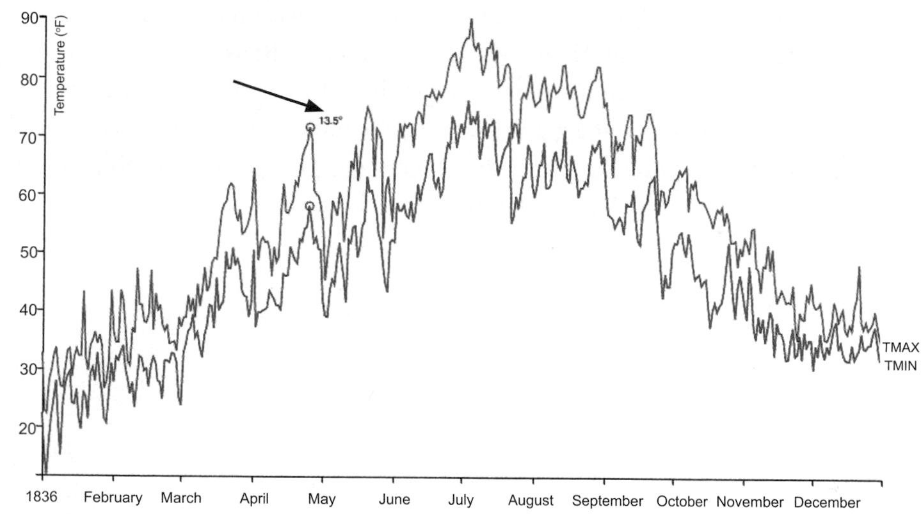

Figure 3.5 Add Temperature Change Value

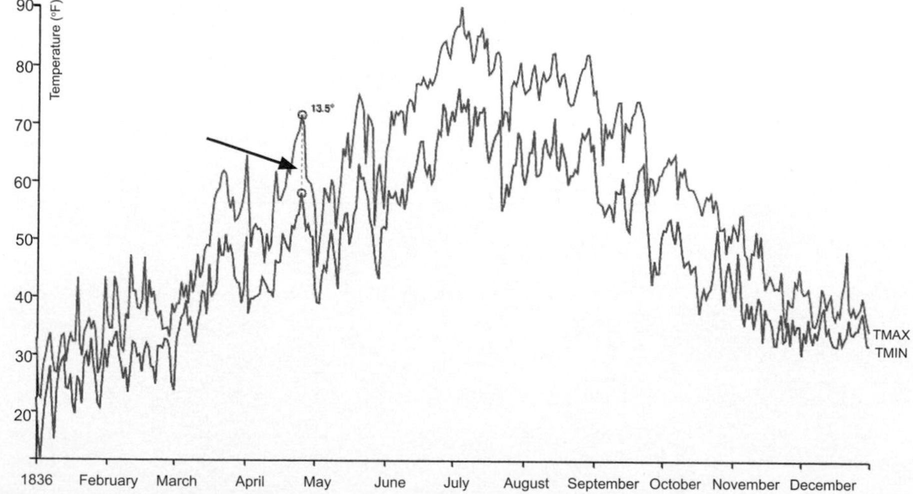

Figure 3.6 Final Daily Minimum/Maximum Temperature Graph

Refresh the page, and, as in Figure 3.6, you should see the finished version with the focal points, temperature change label, and a dotted line between the points.

Code Checkpoint

To see the code at this stage, go to https://github.com/DataVizToolkit/weather/tree/ch03.8.

Summary

In this chapter we looked at a new data set—historic weather readings from the Global Historical Climatology Network. We created a new Rails app for our weather visualizations. We began with a simple line graph and iterated. The initial version was the simplest version of a line graph possible. We took that foundation and made several small updates. I hope that through the series of updates you were able to come to an understanding of how D3 handles data and visual elements.

Chapter 4
Working with Large Datasets

This chapter focuses more on the data than on its presentation. In the real world, data can grow, and it can grow quickly. Being able to work with large data sets and large files that contain the raw data can be a challenge. In this chapter we discuss version control, storage, performance, and benchmarking with large data sets in mind.

Git and Large Files

Git can handle whatever you ask it to handle, including binary files and very large files. Remote hosted Git services, on the other hand, may impose size restrictions. For example, GitHub and Stash limit files to 100 MB.

Before you commit all the things, here are a couple of points to consider. Data files may be a point-in-time snapshot, or only needed to bootstrap or seed the database. For this reason, you may not need or want all files to be version controlled. Will that data file remain useful in a year? If so, then by all means commit it, otherwise consider leaving it out of your version control repository.

Pushing a large file to remote also means that everybody else has to pull that large file, so a friendly heads-up could be helpful.

One solution to the issue of space limitations is Git LFS, also known as `git-lfs`. The "LFS" stands for large file storage. This is a Git extension that must be installed separately. Here is how Git LFS's help describes the extension:

> Git LFS is a system for managing and versioning large files in association with a Git repository. Instead of storing the large files within the Git repository as blobs, Git LFS stores special "pointer files" in the repository, while storing the actual file contents on a Git LFS server. The contents of the large file are downloaded automatically when needed, for example when a Git branch containing the large file is checked out.

> Git LFS works by using a "smudge" filter to look up the large file contents based on the pointer file, and a "clean" filter to create a new version of the pointer file when the large file's contents change. It also uses a pre-push hook to upload the large file contents to the Git LFS server whenever a commit containing a new large file version is about to be pushed to the corresponding Git server.
>
> Like Git, Git LFS commands are separated into high level ("porcelain") commands and low level ("plumbing") commands.

You can use Git LFS locally, and also in conjunction with a remote hosted Git LFS service. GitHub now supports Git LFS. Heroku does not.

Other Git Extensions

There are a handful of other git extensions for handling large files: Git Media, Git Bigstore, and Git Fat are a few. Your mileage may vary with any of these.

If you commit a file that is too large you will need to remove it from Git and your repo's Git history. Look at BFG (https://rtyley.github.io/bfg-repo-cleaner/#usage) and GitHub's Help (https://help.github.com/articles/removing-files-from-a-repository-s-history/) for more on how to remove a file from a repo's history.

The Cloud

Another option for file storage is the cloud. You can put your files in Amazon's S3, Google's gcloud, or a CDN (content delivery network). Some key benefits to hosting files in the cloud are that they don't clutter up your git repo, and the file(s) are not propagated across all of your application server hosts. You can fetch the file via HTTP or the vendor's SDK to load the database.

Hotlinking

You may not need to pull the file down from the remote server at all. All of the data files used in this book are available from data.gov, and we could just read the file directly from the various providers. The downsides to this method are that you maintain open connections from the app server to the remote file and database hosts, and you slurp the entire file into memory.

You could break the process up by pulling the file down using `wget` or `curl`, and then deleting it after the data has been loaded. I would recommend that for larger files. Hotlinking is an option geared more toward smaller files, or when you are constrained on the file system. Listing 4.1 shows an example of a rake task that pulls the 1940 weather data, which is about 14 million records and 500 MB uncompressed, and processes the file in memory.

Listing 4.1 Rake Task to Fetch and Load a Remote Compressed File

```
desc "Fetch and load a remote compressed file"
task :import_noaa_weather_via_http => :environment do
  require 'csv'
  require 'net/http'

  CONN = ActiveRecord::Base.connection
  bulk_insert = lambda { |rows|
    sql = <<-SQL.strip_heredoc
    INSERT INTO weather_readings (station, reading_date, reading_type,
    reading_value, measurement_flag, quality_flag, source_flag,
    observation_time, created_at, updated_at)
    VALUES #{rows.join(',')}
    SQL
    CONN.execute(sql)
  }
  uri =
➥URI("http://www1.ncdc.noaa.gov/pub/data/ghcn/daily/by_year/1940.csv.gz
➥")
  gzip = Net::HTTP.get(uri)
  data = ActiveSupport::Gzip.decompress(gzip)
  rows = []
  n    = 0
  CSV.parse(data) do |row|
    station          = CONN.quote(row[0])
    date_parts       = row[1].match(/(\d{4})(\d{2})(\d{2})/)
    reading_date     = CONN.quote("#{date_parts[1]}-#{date_parts[2]}-
➥#{date_parts[3]}")
    reading_type     = CONN.quote(row[2])
    reading_value    = Integer(row[3])
    measurement_flag = CONN.quote(row[4])
    quality_flag     = CONN.quote(row[5])
    source_flag      = CONN.quote(row[6])
    observation_time = row[7].nil? ? 'NULL' : row[7]
    fields = "(#{station}, #{reading_date}, #{reading_type}, "
    fields += "#{reading_value}, #{measurement_flag}, "
    fields += "#{quality_flag}, #{source_flag}, "
    fields += "#{observation_time}, NOW(), NOW())"
    rows << fields
    n += 1
    if rows.count % 10000 == 0
      bulk_insert.call(rows)
      rows = []
      puts "...#{n} rows added"
```

```
    end
  end
  bulk_insert.call(rows)
  puts "...#{n} rows added"
end
```

Run this rake task (`bundle exec rake db:seed:import_noaa_weather_via_http`) to import the 1940 weather data. It will take some time to run. Alternately you can load the data via `pg_restore` in a fraction of the time.

```
pg_restore -v -c -d weather_development -j3 db/data_files/weather_readings.dump
```

Code Checkpoint

To see the code at this stage, go to https://github.com/DataVizToolkit/weather/tree/ch04.1.

Benchmarking

ActiveRecord provides a helper function, `ActiveRecord::Base.connection#quote`, that will quote strings for you. It is also smart enough to fill in `NULL` values where applicable (instead of an empty string). That's great, and I was happy to find it.

We have a lot of data to read though, and since we are going to call that method a lot we should look at how performant it is. Fortunately, Ruby gives us the ability to run benchmarks in the standard library, so we can answer these sorts of questions. In fact, I have this block in my `.irbrc` file in my home directory so that I can do this easily:

```
require 'benchmark'
def benchmark(n, &block)
  Benchmark.bm do |x|
    x.report do
      n.times { block.call }
    end
  end
end
```

You can invoke that with a one-liner call like this:

```
benchmark(10) { puts 1 }
```

Of course you can also break that into multiple lines and evaluate your real code in the block.

Benchmark and Compare

That benchmark helper is nice, and I use it a lot. You have to do the comparisons yourself, though. Thanks to Evan Phoenix, we have another benchmarking gem that does more detailed comparisons: `benchmark-ips`. You can include the `benchmark-ips` gem in the development and/or test groups in your Gemfile like this:

```
gem 'benchmark-ips', :group => :development
```

Run `bundle install` and then go into the Rails console. With this new tool available, we can do A/B testing like this:

Listing 4.2 Benchmark and Compare String Quoting Methods

```
CONN = ActiveRecord::Base.connection; nil
str = 'foo'
def safe_string(str)
  str.nil? ? 'NULL' : "'#{str}'"
end
Benchmark.ips do |bm|
  bm.report 'ActiveRecord::Base.connection#quote' do
    CONN.quote(str)
  end

  bm.report 'safe_string method' do
    safe_string(str)
  end

  bm.compare!
end
```

Here are the results of the comparison:

```
Calculating -------------------------------------
ActiveRecord::Base.connection#quote
                         8.425k i/100ms
  safe_string method    14.442k i/100ms
-------------------------------------------------
ActiveRecord::Base.connection#quote
                       330.841k (± 9.3%) i/s -      1.643M
  safe_string method      1.394M (±15.3%) i/s -      6.744M

Comparison:
  safe_string method:  1394023.4 i/s
ActiveRecord::Base.connection#quote:   330841.5 i/s - 4.21x slower
```

The results are in, and it doesn't look good for ActiveRecord's helper method. The `quote` method is great, but it does a lot that we don't need. That slows it down, and when we have a large file to parse we want to do it as quickly as possible.

Benchmark All the Things

Know your bottlenecks.

Not every project is going to need high-performance throughput, and that isn't really Ruby's strong suit. However, you should still know when and how to squeeze for higher performance. Any calculation or transformation that you are going to do repeatedly should be evaluated and benchmarked.

Profiling with Ruby Prof

You can get a sense of where your main bottlenecks are by profiling the execution of your code. There are several profiling tools available. A great place to start is the gem `ruby-prof`. Add this to your Gemfile and run `bundle install`:

```
gem 'ruby-prof', :group => :development
```

With the `ruby-prof` gem installed profiling your code is as easy as adding a few additional statements before and after the section that you want to profile. You can profile within the Rails environment, and you can also create a separate little script to profile just a piece of code, like this:

```
require 'ruby-prof'
require 'date'

RubyProf.start

str = "17630104"
date = Date.parse(str)

result = RubyProf.stop
printer = RubyProf::GraphPrinter.new(result)
printer.print(STDOUT)
```

When we run that we see that `Date#parse` is doing a lot of work, including the use of a lot of regular expressions. It needs to figure out what format the date is to know how to parse it. We can do better and cut the string up using a single regular expression. I learned this trick a long time ago (the hard way), and that's why you see the whacky regex in the data load rake tasks.

Benchmarking the Date Parsing

Just so that we know exactly what we are working with here, let's benchmark the date parse methodologies side-by-side. You can run this code in `rails console`:

```
str = "17630104"
Benchmark.ips do |bm|
  bm.report 'Date Parse Regex' do
    date_parts = str.match(/(\d{4})(\d{2})(\d{2})/)
    date = "#{date_parts[1]}-#{date_parts[2]}-#{date_parts[3]}"
  end

  bm.report 'Date#parse' do
    date = Date.parse(str).to_s(:db)
  end

  bm.compare!
end
```

After that runs you get the results:

```
Calculating -------------------------------------
    Date Parse Regex     6.788k i/100ms
          Date#parse     2.311k i/100ms
-------------------------------------------------
    Date Parse Regex    171.007k (±10.1%) i/s -     848.500k
          Date#parse     29.572k (±10.9%) i/s -     145.593k

Comparison:
    Date Parse Regex:   171006.9 i/s
          Date#parse:    29571.6 i/s - 5.78x slower
```

Regular expressions may look like sorcery at times, but as you can see sometimes the additional complexity can be worth it. There are also online tools like http://rubular.com that can help craft your regular expression by testing it in real time.

Code Checkpoint

> To see the code at this stage, go to https://github.com/DataVizToolkit/weather/tree/ch04.2.

Querying "Big Data"

I use the quotes around "big data" because it's such an over-used term now. The NOAA weather data from 1940 does have over 14 million records, though, and that is far from an insignificant amount of data. There are a few things that we need to take into account now to make sure we are as efficient as possible when dealing with these records.

Using Scopes in the Model

We have a long finder method that has several components chained together to fetch the temperature readings, and we've got it in the controller. We should refactor that to the model—in general we want to avoid putting business logic in the controller. The idea is that the controller exists to broker data between the model and the view. Right now the controller is the workhorse, and the model doesn't have any of the domain knowledge.

We can change that by using ActiveRecord scopes, and in doing so make the controller both simpler and flexible. I tend to put these toward the top of my model class below the associations. Add this to the `WeatherReading` model:

```
scope :temps, -> { where(:reading_type => ["TMAX", "TMIN"]) }
scope :with_weather_station, -> { joins(:weather_station) }
scope :with_fields, -> { select("weather_readings.id, reading_date,
➥reading_type, reading_value, source_flag, latitude, longitude,
➥elevation, name") }
scope :for_station, ->(station) { with_weather_station.with_
➥fields.where("weather_stations.name = ?", station) }
scope :sorted, -> { order("reading_type, reading_date") }
scope :for_year, ->(year) { where(:reading_date => Date.new(year,
➥1, 1)..Date.new(year+1, 1, 1)) }
```

There is a lot going on with those six scopes. Refer back to Listing 3.3 to see the original finder method that was in the controller. Here is the new, skinnier, controller.

```
class WeatherController < ApplicationController
  def index; end
  def data
    year     = params[:year] || 1836
    readings =
➥WeatherReading.temps.for_station('MILAN').for_year(year).sorted
    render :json => { :readings => readings }
  end
end
```

You can see that these scopes have greatly simplified the controller. If you look at the `for_station` scope in the model, you can also see that we were able to nest some of the scopes as we defined them.

Another benefit to scopes is that the model now has some domain knowledge. It knows some questions that it will need to be able to answer. We can also ask those questions more easily. We can write tests to make sure that we get the results that we expect, and we can easily run the query in the Rails console.

When we run that query we see that it takes a while to run.

Code Checkpoint

To see the code at this stage, go to https://github.com/DataVizToolkit/weather/tree/ch04.3.

Adding Indices

Not all of the fields that we use to filter the query are indexed. Specifically, in the `weather_readings` table, the `reading_date` and `reading_type` fields are used to filter the query and neither have an index. The same goes for the `name` field in the `weather_stations` table.

You can `EXPLAIN ANALYZE` the query to see how the query optimizer executes the query. When you do that, you'll see that we do a table scan on both tables. That is not good. See Appendix B, "Brief Postgres Overview," for more information on `EXPLAIN ANALYZE` and query planning.

Individual Indices

Postgres has a very good query engine. It can use multiple indices when executing a query. Adding an index is also a very easy thing to do, and we can use an ActiveRecord migration to do it. Create the migration using the Rails generator (`rails g migration add_index_to_weather_readings`):

```
class AddIndexToWeatherReadings < ActiveRecord::Migration
  def change
    add_index :weather_readings, :reading_date
    add_index :weather_readings, :reading_type
  end
end
```

Run the migration (`bundle exec rake db:migrate`). Indexing these fields with over 14 million records in the table will take some time, but it should work without any issues. ActiveRecord migrations may very well be the killer feature of Rails.

Composite Indices

Because the query that we construct will filter results by *both* `reading_date` and `reading_type`, we might be able to benefit from another feature that many databases including Postgres offer: composite indices. These are indices that include multiple columns. We can edit the migration and rerun it. Before we edit it we need to roll it back (`bundle exec rake db:rollback`). That will reverse the migration. Once you've done that you can update the migration to look like this:

```
class AddIndexToWeatherReadings < ActiveRecord::Migration
  def change
    add_index :weather_readings, [:reading_date, :reading_type]
  end
end
```

Using this version of the migration, only a single index will be created. It will still take some time to index all the data.

Code Checkpoint

To see the code at this stage, go to https://github.com/DataVizToolkit/weather/tree/ch04.4.

When Benchmarks and Statistics Lie

All of these techniques for benchmarking and profiling are very helpful, but they can also be a little misleading. Your local development environment is probably fairly different from your staging and production environments.

Your database configuration could be different. Hopefully, your production database is running on a dedicated host. This means the system IO could also be very different. I saw this when benchmarking various implementations of the weather data load rake tasks. Running on the smallest Amazon EC2 instance with a small Amazon RDS Postgres server was twice as fast as running everything on my laptop.

One thing that my laptop has going for it that the Amazon hosts do not is the physical disk. Cloud hosting generally uses networked storage appliances. You do not have a physical disk for your slice of the cloud. As such, you have more latent disk reads.

Those are just a couple of the things that probably differ between your development environment and your production environment. The main thing I want to leave you with is that you really should benchmark all the things—and not just locally in development mode. Use a staging environment, and use realistic data.

Having a realistic expectation of how your code is going to behave before you put it in the wild is invaluable. In a performance-sensitive web app, load testing and code profiling can also help identify bottlenecks. Apache Bench is simple and easy to use for load testing. Ruby-prof and mini-profiler are tools that can profile your code as it runs to help identify bottlenecks.

Of course, problems can still happen, but testing with realistic data on a realistic environment can also help avert crises.

Summary

I covered a lot of different types of information related to working with large data sets in this chapter. It is by no means rigorous or complete. Instead it is intended to shed light on capabilities that you have at your fingertips.

Explore your codebase. Benchmark and profile things that you think might be inefficient. Look at your server logs to see query execution times, and profile those queries.

You don't have to solve all the problems or refactor all the code, but you can take a cut at the worst offender—the least efficient code. It could also save you from kicking off a job that locks up the database, pegs the CPU, or fills up the disk.

Or so I hear.

Part II
Using SQL in Rails

The first section was dedicated to using ActiveRecord for all data access. That works really well for the bulk of what you'll need to do. As your apps grow and the questions you'll need to ask of the data get more complex you may begin to find ActiveRecord starts to get in the way or can't easily do what you need it to do.

In Chapter 5, "Window Functions, Subqueries, and Common Table Expression," we set the foundation for writing raw SQL and discuss user-defined functions, window functions, subqueries, and Common Table Expression. Don't worry if you don't know what those are. You will. We conclude that chapter by building a heatmap to visualize temperatures.

In Chapter 6, "The Chord Diagram," we create a new Rails app for flight departure data and build one of my favorite visualizations—the chord diagram. We continue with the flight departures app in Chapter 7, "Time Series Aggregates in Postgres," where we take a look at utilization for a single airplane—when was it in use and when was it at rest? We build a timeline to see that.

Finally, in Chapter 8, "Using a Separate Reporting Database," we learn how to isolate reporting activity away from regular application activity using a separate database schema to minimize the effect heavy reporting queries have on our users.

Let's get started writing some SQL!

Chapter 5
Window Functions, Subqueries, and Common Table Expression

This is where I start getting really excited! I love Rails, and I love Postgres. In this chapter we teach Postgres how to do new tricks by creating our own functions. We also talk about window functions, which I think are REALLY cool. Before we jump into that, let's talk about mixing the use of raw SQL with an ORM (ActiveRecord in our case). To do this we will bounce between our two applications a little before settling in at the end of the chapter to create a visualization called the heatmap.

Why Use SQL?

This is definitely a troubling subject for some developers. Here's the deal, though. You get to decide what code runs where. Sometimes ActiveRecord gets in the way, or can't do what you want it to do. You've got a powerful database, so use it!

One of the cases for using an ORM is that the query details are abstracted away so you have a more generic interface in your objects. That's great, but the promise of database portability is a bit elusive.

Database Portability Is a Lie

When was the last time that you migrated an application from one database type to a different database type? In the 15 years or so that I've been programming I've done it a few times. It is not as simple as just changing the gem and `database.yml` configuration file. Not even close.

Different databases have different features. They have different data types. They handle sorting differently (for example, nulls at the beginning or end of the results).

They handle timestamps differently. Postgres timestamps have microseconds where MySQL cannot get any more granular than the second.

If you're migrating to a different database, or even upgrading major versions, there is a pretty good chance that you're going to need to write something to help make the transition. I have not done a database changeover where I didn't have to do a lot of handholding, even when using a tool written specifically for the migration.

So if we take the promise of database portability off the table, an ORM ends up being a tool to abstract away the nitty gritty connection details and make it easy to interact with data in an OO manner. ActiveRecord (the gem) implements Active Record (the pattern). That just means that it stores data from a relational database in memory and understands how to translate (persist) CRUD (Create, Read, Update, Delete) operations from the in-memory object down to the database.

I should note here that in Rails not all objects need to be persisted in the database. It is absolutely OK to have a model that does not live in the database.

Tripping Over ActiveRecord

Let's look at two examples from the "Joining Tables" section of the Active Record Query Interface Guide (http://guides.rubyonrails.org/active_record_querying.html). Can you look at this and tell what is going on?

```
Category.joins(:articles)
```

That seems simple enough, right? We are going to join articles and categories together. If the relations are specified in the models, ActiveRecord knows the foreign key to join on. Here is the SQL that is generated for that statement.

```
SELECT categories.* FROM categories
  INNER JOIN articles ON articles.category_id = categories.id
```

What about this?

```
Article.joins(comments: :guest)
```

You have to think a little harder on that one, don't you? Article joins to comments, which joins to guests. Again, the relations are defined in the models, so ActiveRecord knows the proper foreign keys. I also must confess that I prefer the older hashrocket style for writing hash key/value. The kissing colons look strange to me. I digress. Here is that SQL.

```
SELECT articles.* FROM articles
  INNER JOIN comments ON comments.article_id = articles.id
  INNER JOIN guests ON guests.comment_id = comments.id
```

So far we are doing pretty well. We've had to think a little harder with that second example, but not too hard. What about this example?

```
Category.joins(articles: [{ comments: :guest }, :tags])
```

Hmmmm. I don't really know what the expected behavior of all that is without looking it up. The documentation says this is a nested join, so we are building a chain of joins. That query is starting to get pretty large and complicated. Here is what the generated SQL actually looks like.

```
SELECT categories.* FROM categories
  INNER JOIN articles ON articles.category_id = categories.id
  INNER JOIN comments ON comments.article_id = articles.id
  INNER JOIN guests ON guests.comment_id = comments.id
  INNER JOIN tags ON tags.article_id = articles.id
```

I urge you to be thoughtful about your database queries. When you start generating complex SQL statements with ActiveRecord consider that it may be worthwhile to simplify and just write the SQL queries. I don't know about you, but I had to stop and think on that second example. I had to go to the documentation on the third example. Yuck.

Future you and other future developers will thank you for being clear and not making them work harder than necessary to follow the intention of the code.

You can see more information on joins in Appendix C, "SQL Join Overview."

User-Defined Functions

Right. So now that we've covered some of the rationale behind why it's OK to break away from the comfort of ActiveRecord to write raw SQL, let's go ahead and kick over another sacred cow.

You can teach Postgres new tricks. You do this by creating your own functions. What's a function, you ask? In other databases it may be called a Stored Procedure. These user-defined functions simply "execute an arbitrary list of SQL statements" according to the Postgres documentation.

Why?

You would generally do this when you need to calculate a value with a complex formula. You can also execute a basic query in a function, but that's not actually the most performant way to tackle that. Refer to Appendix B, "Brief Postgres Overview," for information on Views and Materialized Views to read more about that.

Heresy!

Yes, I know suggesting that you break business logic out of your application and stuff it into the database is heretical. I am not suggesting that you put ALL of your business logic in the database. I am saying this is a tool that you have at your disposal, and sometimes you may find it useful.

How?

Here is an example of a very simple, and admittedly contrived, example from the Postgres documentation. The `$$` is another way to quote strings in Postgres.

```
CREATE FUNCTION one() RETURNS integer AS $$
    SELECT 1 AS result;
$$ LANGUAGE SQL;

SELECT one();

 one
-----
   1
```

All this function does is return a single one. It is the loneliest function, isn't it? We would never need this, but maybe we *would* want to calculate a number. The weird dollar signs are quotes.

In the residential sales data we have average home sales amounts. I wonder what the mortgage payments would look like for those neighborhoods. The formula to calculate that is

$$c = \frac{rP}{1-(1+r)^{-N}}$$

- r is the **monthly** interest rate
- N is number of monthly payments (the loan's term)
- P is the borrowed amount (the principal)

That's kind of a hassle to put inline in the SQL. We could calculate it in the Rails app, and maybe that works fine for your use case. What if we wanted to filter the query based on that calculation, though? I actually had a project where I needed to do just that.

We can do this calculation easily in the database. We just need to create a new function to do it. Don't worry, it's not as scary as it sounds at first. We'll create the migration soon, but first let's take a look at the function.

```
CREATE OR REPLACE FUNCTION pmt(
  interest double precision,
  principal integer)
RETURNS numeric AS $$
  SELECT ROUND(CAST((interest/100/12 * principal) / (1 - ((1 +
➥(interest/100/12)) ^ -360)) AS numeric), 0)
$$ LANGUAGE SQL;
```

I used `CREATE OR REPLACE` this time. You'd get an error from Postgres if you tried to run the migration and the function already existed. This is also how you could update the function. Note that the function name is defined *with* the parameter types. So that function is referred to as `pmt(double precision, integer)`.

Getting the mortgage payment with the rest of the data is as easy as including it in the query. Actually, let's see what the 5 most expensive zip codes were. We can jump into the Postgres psql console by running `rails dbconsole`. See Appendix B, "Brief Postgres Overview," for more on SQL editors.

```
SELECT id, year, jurisdiction, zipcode, median_value, pmt(4.25, median_value::int)
FROM sales_figures
WHERE median_value > 999
ORDER BY 3, 6
LIMIT 5;
```

We stored `median_value` as a float (double precision), so we need to recast it to an integer because that's what `pmt(double precision, integer)` expects for the principal. You may wonder why bother with the extra step of changing the type? The principal amount in a mortgage calculation is generally a whole number. The negotiated price of real estate is not typically "and 27 cents." The data, however, is a calculated median. The pennies are considered a rounding error and not significant, so it is safe to recast the median value as an integer. If we did not recast to an integer Postgres would complain, telling us that there is no function `pmt(double precision, double precision)`.

We can order the results by field name, but also by the position of the field (or value) in the query. That works really well when we have a calculated field that would otherwise have to be restated. Just be sure that you update the sort order if you change the order or number of fields in the query.

Here are the results from the query, in case you were curious.

```
 id  | year | jurisdiction | zipcode | total_sales | median_value | pmt
-----+------+--------------+---------+-------------+--------------+-----
 277 | 2012 | Montgomery   | 20818   |          24 |       933500 | 4592
 398 | 2012 | Talbot       | 21662   |          10 |       890000 | 4378
 274 | 2012 | Montgomery   | 20815   |         301 |       825000 | 4059
 243 | 2012 | Howard       | 20777   |          36 |       797500 | 3923
 288 | 2012 | Montgomery   | 20854   |         511 |       797000 | 3921
(5 rows)
```

How to Use SQL in Rails

Using raw SQL in Rails is actually quite easy. We can also create a migration to create the `pmt(double precision, integer)` function. Database migrations may be my absolute favorite thing about Rails.

```
rails g migration CreatePMTFunction
```

The default migration assumes you want to create a new table. That's not what we need in this case. This is not a reversible migration, so we need to specify how to handle both the creation (`up`) as well as the teardown (`down`) of the function. Here is the updated migration:

```
class CreatePmtFunction < ActiveRecord::Migration
  def up
    # Create the pmt function
    sql = <<-SQL.strip_heredoc
    CREATE OR REPLACE FUNCTION pmt(
      interest double precision,
      principal integer)
    RETURNS numeric AS $$
      SELECT ROUND(
        CAST(
          (interest/100/12 * principal)
          / (1 - ((1 + (interest/100/12)) ^ -360))
        AS numeric), 0)
    $$ LANGUAGE SQL;
    SQL
    execute(sql)
  end

  def down
    # Drop the pmt function
    execute("DROP FUNCTION pmt(double precision, integer);")
  end
end
```

execute is a shortcut for ActiveRecord::Base.connection.execute. You could write it all out, and that would be fine. I also added a little syntactic sugar with the strip_heredoc. That's a neat trick that strips off the leading spaces from the SQL so that when it's printed to the log (or STDOUT) it's a little more legible.

There is one more thing you're going to want to change now that we've created our own function. When you run the migration you see that the only thing that changed in the schema.rb file is the schema version at the top of the file. There is no record of the new function. We need the schema dump to reflect all of our database objects. Your tests load the db/schema.rb or db/structure.sql file when they run.

What is that structure.sql file you ask? The Ruby schema file is meant to handle the most basic database objects across all databases. We have ventured off that path, so we need to switch to the SQL version that can properly express all of our database objects. Add this line to your config/application.rb file:

```
config.active_record.schema_format = :sql
```

Now when you run your migrations, or if you run the db:structure:dump rake task, you'll generate the db/structure.sql file. You can safely delete the db/schema.rb file. You don't need it anymore.

Scatter Plot with Mortgage Payment

Now that we can calculate the mortgage payment, let's revise the scatter plot to show those values. The first thing I want to do is take the query from earlier in the chapter and drop that into the SalesFigure model.

```
def self.mortgage_payment_data
  sql = <<-SQL.strip_heredoc
    SELECT id, year, jurisdiction, zipcode, total_sales,
      median_value, pmt(4.25, median_value::int)
    FROM sales_figures
    WHERE median_value > 999
    ORDER BY 3, 6;
  SQL
  connection.execute(sql)
end
```

Now we can run that query in the console and also in the controller. If you run it in the console, you'll see that you get back a PG::Result object. You can do all the things you'd want to with that. It's just an array of hashes.

```
>> data = SalesFigure.mortgage_payment_data
   (12.6ms)  SELECT id, year, jurisdiction, zipcode, total_sales,
➥median_value, pmt(4.25, median_value::int)
```

```
FROM sales_figures
WHERE median_value > 999
ORDER BY 3, 6

=> #<PG::Result:0x007ff7c1b00458 status=PGRES_TUPLES_OK ntuples=383
➥nfields=6 cmd_tuples=383>
>> data.first
=> {"id"=>"5", "year"=>"2012", "jurisdiction"=>"Allegany",
➥"zipcode"=>"21539", "total_sales"=>"8", "median_value"=>"66500",
➥"pmt"=>"327"}
>> data.count
=> 383
```

Because we've sidestepped ActiveRecord to run our query, we don't get any of the benefits that it brings to the table. All the values in the result set are strings because we don't get any of the type coercion that ActiveRecord normally does on our model's fields.

We can now simplify the `scatter_data` controller method.

```
def scatter_data
  data = SalesFigure.mortgage_payment_data
  render :json => { :scatter_data => data }
end
```

Now we just need to make two small changes in the `makeScatter()` function to coerce the values to numeric and change out the `median_value` for the calculated `pmt` field.

```
var xValue = function(d) { return +d.total_sales;}
```

And also

```
var yValue = function(d) { return +d.pmt;}
```

The + that precedes the returned values in those functions is a D3 convenience function to coerce a string into a number. You could also use the JavaScript `parseInt` function.

The revised scatter plot has the same distribution of values. The values are just a lot lower. See Figure 5.1 for the updated scatter plot.

Code Checkpoint

To see the code at this stage, go to https://github.com/DataVizToolkit/residential_sales/tree/ch05.1.

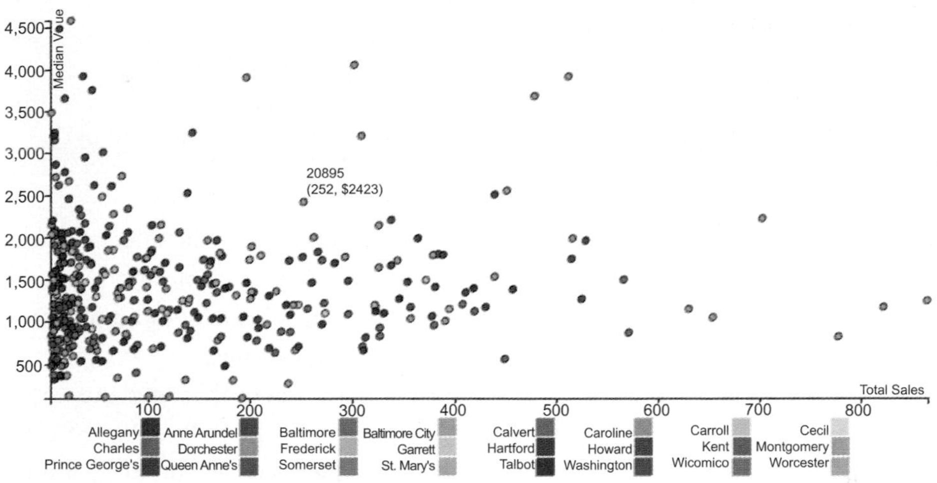

Figure 5.1 Scatter Plot with Mortgage Payment

Window Functions

Window functions are not unique to Postgres, but they're one of the things that excite me the most in Postgres. In fact, this is what I led off with in the RailsConf talk that launched this book (http://confreaks.tv/videos/railsconf2015-making-data-dance). The Postgres documentation defines window functions as follows:

> A *window function* performs a calculation across a set of table rows that are somehow related to the current row. This is comparable to the type of calculation that can be done with an aggregate function. But unlike regular aggregate functions, use of a window function does not cause rows to become grouped into a single output row—the rows retain their separate identities. Behind the scenes, the window function is able to access more than just the current row of the query result.

The Postgres documentation is usually pretty good. That definition describes exactly what a window function is—some calculation performed across a set of records and placed in the current record. In other words, you're folding data from other rows into the current row.

Window Functions Greatest Hits

There are 11 window functions available in Postgres. Five of them are what I call the "greatest hits" of Postgres window functions. They are:

- `lead()`
- `lag()`

- `first_value()`
- `last_value()`
- `row_number()`

Lead and Lag

Have you ever wished that you could look ahead (or behind) to see the value of a field in the next (or previous) record? You could write logic in your application to hold onto the previous value as you iterate over the results, but that's a lot of unnecessary processing when you can just have the database give you the values.

Let's jump back to the weather app and see what a query that uses the `lead` window function looks like. Type the following query into the SQL editor of your choice (e.g., pgAdmin or `rails dbconsole`). This query will let you easily distinguish whether the temperature went up or down from one day to the next for each weather station.

You could add an index on `station` before running the query. It will still table scan, but it will execute a little faster.

```
SELECT id, station, reading_date, reading_value,
  lead(reading_value) OVER (PARTITION BY station ORDER BY reading_date) AS
➥next_reading_value
FROM weather_readings
WHERE reading_type = 'TMAX'
LIMIT 5;
   id   |   station   | reading_date | reading_value | next_reading_value
--------+-------------+--------------+---------------+--------------------
  17959 | AG000060390 | 1940-01-01   |           224 |                202
  56896 | AG000060390 | 1940-01-02   |           202 |                210
  95806 | AG000060390 | 1940-01-03   |           210 |                191
 134782 | AG000060390 | 1940-01-04   |           191 |                175
 173950 | AG000060390 | 1940-01-05   |           175 |                173
 (5 rows)
```

Partitions

There was a little more going on in that query that I hadn't mentioned yet. Let's take another look at the Postgres documentation to see what's happening.

> A window function call always contains an `OVER` clause directly following the window function's name and argument(s). This is what syntactically distinguishes it from a regular function or aggregate function. The `OVER` clause determines exactly how the rows of the query are split up for processing by the window function. The `PARTITION BY` list within `OVER` specifies dividing the rows into groups, or partitions, that share

the same values of the PARTITION BY expression(s). For each row, the window function is computed across the rows that fall into the same partition as the current row.

So really, the function is LEAD(field) OVER(). You can omit the partition, and Postgres will use the full table as the partition.

First Value and Last Value

The next pair of window functions in my Top 5 list helps you see the first or last value in the partitions. This is particularly helpful when you need to look at change events. For example, imagine you've got a series of location readings as you move around a building. You could have several readings in a room, then more readings in another room. You want to know when you moved from one room to the next.

```
SELECT id, room,
  first_value (id) OVER (PARTITION BY room ORDER BY id) AS entrance_id
FROM readings
```

The first_value() would be your entrance into each room.

Row Number

The final window function in my Top 5 list tells you the number of the current row within its partition. For this example, we are back in the residential sales app. Type this query into the SQL editor of your choice.

```
SELECT id, jurisdiction, zipcode, median_value,
  row_number() OVER(PARTITION BY jurisdiction ORDER BY median_value)
FROM sales_figures
WHERE median_value > 999
LIMIT 10;
```

```
 id | jurisdiction   | zipcode | median_value | row_number
----+----------------+---------+--------------+------------
  5 | Allegany       | 21539   |        66500 |          1
  7 | Allegany       | 21555   |        74000 |          2
  9 | Allegany       | 21562   |        76000 |          3
  1 | Allegany       | 21502   |        98242 |          4
  8 | Allegany       | 21557   |       107750 |          5
  4 | Allegany       | 21532   |       110000 |          6
  3 | Allegany       | 21530   |       113500 |          7
 43 | Anne Arundel   | 21225   |       182274 |          1
 32 | Anne Arundel   | 21061   |       217695 |          2
 44 | Anne Arundel   | 21226   |       217950 |          3
(10 rows)
```

The `row_number()` looks like it could also be a rank order value, and it sort of is. There is a subtle difference, though, but we need a slightly more sophisticated query to highlight it.

Using Subqueries

You can nest a query inside another query. Why would you want to do this, you ask? You can filter a query by selecting from it. For example, I want to see all the records where the `row_number()` and `rank()` window functions differ. `rank()` is generally the same as `row_number()` except that where values are equal the rank is equal—like two people being in first place.

The query looks like this:

```
SELECT * FROM (
  SELECT id, jurisdiction, zipcode, median_value,
    rank() OVER(PARTITION BY jurisdiction ORDER BY median_value),
    row_number() OVER(PARTITION BY jurisdiction ORDER BY median_value)
  FROM sales_figures
  WHERE median_value > 999
) AS subq
WHERE rank <> row_number;
```

```
 id  |   jurisdiction    | zipcode | median_value | rank | row_number
-----+-------------------+---------+--------------+------+------------
  95 | Baltimore         | 21244   |       178250 |    9 |         10
 256 | Howard            | 21723   |       660000 |   19 |         20
 289 | Montgomery        | 20855   |       405000 |   19 |         20
 347 | Prince George's   | 20785   |       145000 |    8 |          9
 419 | Washington        | 21795   |       192500 |    7 |          8
(5 rows)
```

We've wrapped the main query in another query that limits the results to *just* the records where the `rank` and `row_number` differ. From there you could run a query to look specifically at one of those jurisdiction if you wanted to see the specifics.

The subquery is named, and you could refer to the fields from the subquery with that namespace if you needed to specify them. I called the subquery `subq`, but you could name it whatever or however was most meaningful in your situation.

Common Table Expression

There is another way to write the subquery that makes it easier to read and also composable called Common Table Expression (CTE). You may also see CTE referred to as a `WITH` query. Here is what the Postgres documentation has to say about `WITH` queries:

> `WITH` provides a way to write auxiliary statements for use in a larger query. These statements, which are often referred to as Common Table Expressions or CTEs, can be thought of as defining temporary tables that exist just for one query.

The nested query would be rewritten as follows

```
WITH subq AS (
  SELECT id, jurisdiction, zipcode, median_value,
    rank() OVER(PARTITION BY jurisdiction ORDER BY median_value),
    row_number() OVER(PARTITION BY jurisdiction ORDER BY median_value)
  FROM sales_figures
  WHERE median_value > 999
)
SELECT * FROM subq WHERE rank <> row_number;
```

The results are exactly the same.

Note

If you are unfamiliar with the `<>` operator, that is the ANSI SQL standard for "not equal." Postgres supports both `<>` and `!=` for not equal. I actually use both, but the greater than and less than keys are closer to each other and easier for me to type.

The real benefit with CTE is the legibility as you compose more complicated queries. Let's look and see which zip codes are the most expensive in each jurisdiction.

```
WITH subq AS (
  SELECT id, jurisdiction, zipcode, median_value,
    row_number() OVER(PARTITION BY jurisdiction ORDER BY median_value
➥DESC)
  FROM sales_figures
  WHERE median_value > 999
), most_expensive_zipcodes AS (
  SELECT * FROM subq WHERE row_number = 1
)
SELECT id, jurisdiction, zipcode, median_value
FROM most_expensive_zipcodes
ORDER BY median_value;
```

```
 id  |   jurisdiction    | zipcode | median_value
-----+-------------------+---------+--------------
   3 | Allegany          | 21530   |       113500
 425 | Wicomico          | 21830   |       172450
 110 | Caroline          | 21629   |       180450
 385 | Somerset          | 21821   |       192500
```

```
 413 | Washington       | 21756    |        236822
[snip]
  27 | Anne Arundel     | 21035    |        612500
  80 | Baltimore        | 21210    |        655100
 243 | Howard           | 20777    |        797500
 398 | Talbot           | 21662    |        890000
 277 | Montgomery       | 20818    |        933500
(24 rows)
```

CTE and the Heatmap

A heatmap is an interesting visualization for a grid of information. The data could be hourly data from several different sensors, where each sensor would be represented as a row in the grid and the hours as columns. You can also show a calendar as a heatmap, like the [in]famous GitHub contribution graph.

We have weather data, so let's see what a heatmap would look like for temperatures—a heatmap of heat, if you will.

The Query

Since we are making a heatmap of daily data, we are essentially making a colorful calendar. The first thing that we need to make a calendar is the daily data. Let's go back to the weather app. Here is a CTE query that creates daily max temperature readings. I've added this in a class method in the `WeatherReading` model.

```
def self.heatmap(station)
  sql = <<-SQL.strip_heredoc
    WITH days AS (
      SELECT dt
      FROM generate_series(
        '18360101'::timestamp, '18361231'::timestamp, '1 day'
      ) AS dt
    ), temperature_readings AS (
      SELECT id, reading_date, reading_value
      FROM weather_readings
      WHERE reading_type = 'TMAX'
        AND station = '#{station}'
      ORDER BY 2
    )
    SELECT tr.*
    FROM temperature_readings tr
    RIGHT JOIN days ON reading_date >= days.dt AND reading_date <=
➥days.dt;
  SQL
  connection.execute(sql)
end
```

This query builds up two separate queries and then uses a `RIGHT JOIN` to merge them together. The first query (`days`) uses the Postgres `generate_series` function to generate 365 days, one for each day in 1836. I do this because you can never assume that your data is any good. There could be missing days, and I want every day represented in the data.

The second query (`temperature_readings`) pulls out all the maximum temperature values for the given station and sorts them by `reading_date`. The `RIGHT JOIN` then takes all of the days that we generated and includes any temperature reading records that meet the join criteria. In this case it happens to be all of the readings, which is nice.

The Controller and View

The next thing we should do is create the controller actions.

```
def heatmap; end
def heatmap_data
  data = WeatherReading.heatmap('ITE00100554')
  render :json => data
end
```

Next, we need to create the views and routes. We can copy the index view file from Chapter 3, "Working with Time Series Data," to `app/views/weather/heatmap.html.erb` and change it like we've been doing. The JavaScript function that we are going to call is `makeHeatMap()`, so update `heatmap.html.erb` to call that function.

The routes that we need are:

```
get 'weather/heatmap'
get 'weather/heatmap_data', :defaults => { :format => 'json' }
```

Finally, we need to add a little more CSS to style the heatmap.

```
// Heatmap
.day {
  fill: #fff;
  stroke: #ccc;
}

.month {
  fill: none;
  stroke: #000;
  stroke-width: 2px;
}
```

The JavaScript

The last thing we need to do is write the JavaScript to generate the chart. I found an example that looked at financial data for several years (http://bl.ocks.org/mbostock/4063318). It's not exactly what we need, but it's a good start.

We are looking at temperatures, and the `reading_value` that we get out of the database needs to be converted. This is the second chart where we need to do that, so I've extracted that calculation out of `makeLineChart()` and created a separate function for it.

```
function fahrenheit(celcius) {
  return +celcius * 0.1 * 9/5 + 32;
}
```

The plus sign before the parameter is a convenience function provided by D3 to coerce a string into a number.

With the `fahrenheit` function in place, we are ready to draw our calendar heatmap. Listing 5.1 shows the code. You can see the finished product in Figure 5.2.

Listing 5.1 Heatmap JavaScript

```
function makeHeatMap() {
  var width    = 960,
      height   = 136,
      cellSize = 17, // cell size
      // blue, green, yellow, orange, red
      colors   = ['#0000FF', '#00FF00', '#FFFF00', '#FFA500', '#FF0000'],
      format   = d3.time.format("%Y-%m-%d"),
      decimal  = d3.format(".1f");

  // draw the year(s)
  var svg = d3.select("body").selectAll("svg")
      .data(d3.range(1836, 1837))
    .enter().append("svg")
      .attr("width", width)
      .attr("height", height)
      .attr("class", "RdYlGn")
    .append("g")
```

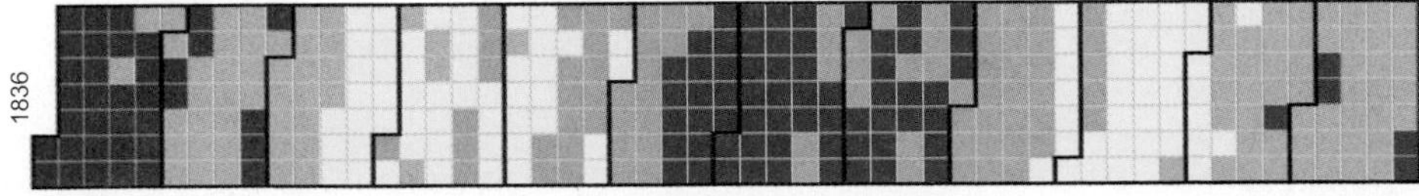

Figure 5.2 TMAX Heatmap

```
      .attr("transform", "translate(" + ((width - cellSize * 53) / 2) +
➥"," + (height - cellSize * 7 - 1) + ")");

  // year label to the left of the calendar
  svg.append("text")
      .attr("transform", "translate(-6," + cellSize * 3.5 + ")rotate(-
➥90)")
      .style("text-anchor", "middle")
      .text(function(d) { return d; });

  // fill in the calendar(s)
  var rect = svg.selectAll(".day")
      .data(function(d) { return d3.time.days(new Date(d, 0, 1),
➥new Date(d + 1, 0, 1)); })
    .enter().append("rect")
      .attr("class", "day")
      .attr("width", cellSize)
      .attr("height", cellSize)
      .attr("x", function(d) { return d3.time.weekOfYear(d) * cellSize;
➥})
      .attr("y", function(d) { return d.getDay() * cellSize; })
      .datum(format);

  // mouseover title
  rect.append("title")
      .text(function(d) { return d; });

  var monthPath = function(t0) {
    var t1 = new Date(t0.getFullYear(), t0.getMonth() + 1, 0),
        d0 = t0.getDay(), w0 = d3.time.weekOfYear(t0),
        d1 = t1.getDay(), w1 = d3.time.weekOfYear(t1);
    return "M" + (w0 + 1) * cellSize + "," + d0 * cellSize
        + "H" + w0 * cellSize + "V" + 7 * cellSize
        + "H" + w1 * cellSize + "V" + (d1 + 1) * cellSize
        + "H" + (w1 + 1) * cellSize + "V" + 0
        + "H" + (w0 + 1) * cellSize + "Z";
  }

  // darker line to separate the months of the year
  svg.selectAll(".month")
      .data(function(d) { return d3.time.months(new Date(d, 0, 1), new
➥Date(d + 1, 0, 1)); })
    .enter().append("path")
      .attr("class", "month")
      .attr("d", monthPath);

  d3.json('/weather/heatmap_data.json', function(error, readings) {
    var data = [],
```

```
      min  = Infinity,
      max  = -Infinity;
    readings.forEach(function(reading) {
      // type coersions and temperature conversion
      var temperature = fahrenheit(reading.reading_value);
      data[reading.reading_date] = {
        id          : +reading.id,
        temperature : temperature,
        date        : new Date(reading.reading_date),
      };
      if (temperature < min) { min = temperature }
      if (temperature > max) { max = temperature }
    });

    var color = d3.scale.quantize().domain([min, max]).range(colors);

    rect.filter(function(key) { return key in data; })
        .style("fill", function(key) { return
➥color(data[key].temperature); })
      .select("title")
        .text(function(key) { return key + ": " +
➥decimal(data[key].temperature); });
  });
}
```

I didn't actually need to change too much from the original example. The main differences are the color scale and how I process the data.

When you go to http://localhost:3000/weather/heatmap it will take a moment for the colors to fill in. The finished graph looks like what you might expect. The coldest days were in January, and the hottest days were late June through August.

Code Checkpoint

To see the code at this stage, go to https://github.com/DataVizToolkit/weather/tree/ch05.1.

Summary

In this chapter I started making the case for when it's OK to venture away from the conveniences that ActiveRecord provides. Don't get me wrong, I love ActiveRecord. It just gets in the way sometimes. Complex joins, for example, are probably easier to write (and also read) in raw SQL.

There are also more complex queries and deeper database functionality for which you need to use raw SQL to fully utilize them, such as user-defined functions and window functions. We created a function to calculate mortgage payment values and updated the scatter plot to use our custom function.

We will spend a little more time with window functions soon, but I wanted to introduce them to you and also use them to show you how subqueries and Common Table Expression (CTE) work.

Finally, we used CTE as the basis for a heatmap.

CHAPTER 6
The Chord Diagram

A chord diagram, also known as a radial network diagram, is a circular diagram with arcs (chords) that connect related points around a circle to show relationships among a group of entities. A chord diagram can be very visually appealing. It is one of my favorite data visualizations. I am very excited to walk through the creation of one with you. You can see an example of a chord diagram in Figure 6.1.

The Matrix Is the Truth

In order to define the relations between all the points, the chord diagram requires the input data be in a special format called a square matrix. An example square matrix is provided in the D3 documentation (https://github.com/d3/d3/wiki/Chord-Layout):

```
[[11975,  5871, 8916, 2868],
 [ 1951, 10048, 2060, 6171],
 [ 8010, 16145, 8090, 8045],
 [ 1013,   990,  940, 6907]]
```

Each category (group) gets a row in the matrix. Each column index corresponds to a category in that index's row. Each row shows the relationship of an entity to each entity in the list. Cell [0][3] gives us the relationship of the first entity to the fourth entity. If this data represented flight departures, then there are 2868 flights that departed from Airport 0 and arrived at Airport 3.

I will talk more about generating the matrix a little later in this chapter. First let's have a look at the data and set up a new Rails app.

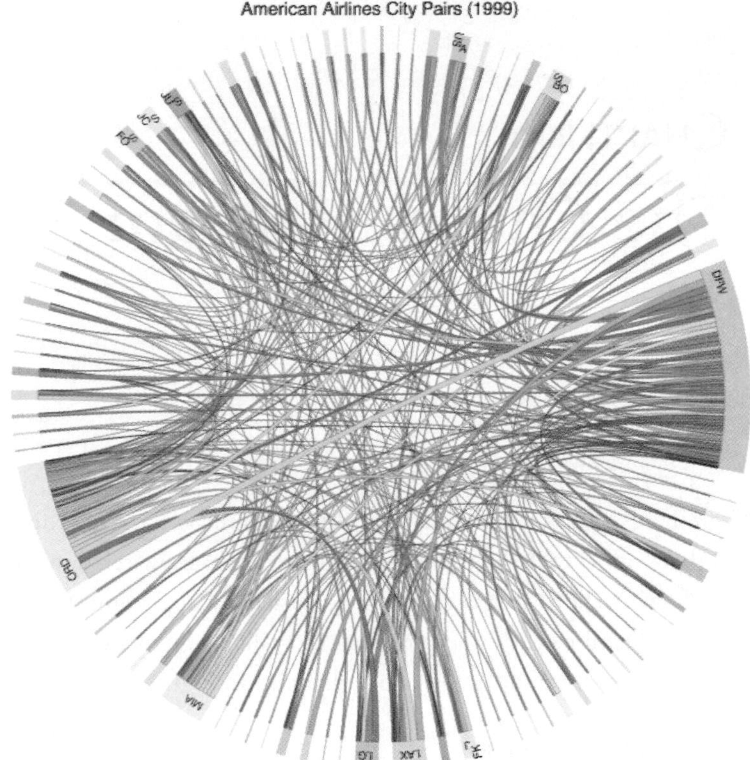

Figure 6.1 Example Chord Diagram.

Flight Departures Data

We are going to look at flight departures and diagram the origin and destination city-pairs. The Bureau of Transportation Statistics (BTS) has a lot of interesting transportation data. The American Statistical Association (ASA) had a contest a few years ago that used flight data from the BTS. The ASA cleaned the files up a little and provided a data dictionary. We will use the ASA's version of the data, which you can find at http://stat-computing.org/dataexpo/2009/the-data.html

You could get more recent data directly from BTS, but I'm going to use the oldest data I can find that includes airplane tail numbers. You'll see why that is important shortly. Download the data set from 1999.

There are two other files that we also want, which can be found at http://stat-computing.org/dataexpo/2009/supplemental-data.html. Download the airport and carrier CSV files.

Departures App

Now that you have the data files it's time to start working on the app. Create a new Rails app that uses Postgres as the database:

```
rails new departures --skip-bundle -d postgresql
```

You can look in Appendix A, "Ruby and Rails Setup," for more information on how I generally create and configure a new Rails app. Create a new folder, `db/data_files`, move the two CSV files in there, and don't forget to run `rake db:create`.

Code Checkpoint

To see the code at this stage, go to https://github.com/DataVizToolkit/departures/tree/ch06.1.

Airports

Before we dive into the departures, we need to load some of the related data. As you surely know, a flight begins and ends at an airport. We will use the file provided with the data challenge to load our airports.

Generate the Model

Create the `Airport` model and migration as follows:

```
rails generate model airport iata:string{4}:uniq airport \
  city state country lat:float long:float
```

That will give you an `Airport` model and also the migration to create the `airports` table. We specify that we want the length of the `iata` field to be no more than 4 characters, and we also want to index that field.

Load the Data

There are a lot of airports, but the data file is not very large. We can use Ruby's built-in CSV library to read and convert the data, and we can use ActiveRecord to create new records. I use the same sort of rake task as in previous chapters, namespaced in the `db:seed` namespace.

I am generally not a fan of using "`long`" as an abbreviation for longitude, but that is what was in the data file. For this file and the next I wanted to keep the field names and header names in sync so that I could show the header converter in action. It takes the header field, downcases it, and then symbolizes it. The beauty of that is that you can take the row as you read it in and convert it to a hash that ActiveRecord understands in a `create` statement. The keys do not need to be converted to symbols for ActiveRecord to understand them, but I like my keys as symbols.

```
require 'csv'
CSV::Converters[:blank_to_nil] = lambda do |field|
  field && field.empty? ? nil : field
end

namespace :db do
  namespace :seed do
    desc "Import airport data"
    task :import_airports => :environment do
      if Airport.count == 0
        filename     = Rails.root.join('db', 'data_files',
➥'airports.csv')
        fixed_quotes = File.read(filename).gsub(/\\"/,'""')
        CSV.parse(fixed_quotes, :headers => true, :header_converters =>
➥:symbol, :converters => [:blank_to_nil]) do |row|
          Airport.create(row.to_hash)
        end
      end
    end
  end
end
```

The really cool thing here is that the CSV library can understand how to do simple transformations as it reads the data. It can automatically convert fields to integer (any field that `Integer()` would accept), float (any field `Float()` accepts), date (`Date::parse()`), datetime (`DateTime::parse()`), and any combination of these. You can also create your own in addition to what the standard library offers, which is what we do with `:blank_to_nil`.

We also needed to clean the data a little before we could feed it into CSV. The CSV library expects quotes that are within strings to be escaped differently than the way they were escaped in the data. CSV will consider a double sequence of the quote character to be an escaped quote.

Carriers

The `carriers.csv` file is the list of all the airlines. There are a lot of airlines, but the CSV file is not too large. This airline file also works nicely with the departure data.

Generate the Model

This model is a lot simpler with only two fields. We do the same sort of thing that we did for Airports:

```
rails g model carrier code:string{7}:uniq description
```

Load the Data

The carrier file is also not a very large file, so we can use CSV and ActiveRecord again to load the data.

```
desc "Import airline/carrier data"
task :import_carriers => :environment do
  if Carrier.count == 0
    filename = Rails.root.join('db', 'data_files', 'carriers.csv')
    CSV.foreach(filename, :headers => true, :header_converters =>
➥:symbol) do |row|
      Carrier.create(row.to_hash)
    end
  end
end
```

We can run the migration and rake task together:

```
bundle exec rake db:migrate db:seed:import_carriers
```

Code Checkpoint

To see the code at this stage, go to https://github.com/DataVizToolkit/departures/tree/ch06.2.

Departures

The last file you need to grab, if you haven't already, is the 1999 departures data (http://stat-computing.org/dataexpo/2009/the-data.html). The DataExpo site gives a nice database schema for a SQLite database. Even though we are using Postgres, we can still use that for guidance. Unfortunately, the data is not clean. The Airline IATA code (UniqueCarrier) is sometimes too long for the field. Rather than modify the data, we will make the field long enough to support the data.

Generate the Model

There are a lot of fields, and there is a lot of data. We are going to need to do things a little differently here. We will create the model and migration using this generator:

```
rails g model departure year:integer:index month:integer \
  day_of_month:integer day_of_week:integer dep_time:integer \
  crs_dep_time:integer arr_time:integer crs_arr_time:integer \
  unique_carrier:string{6}:index flight_num:integer \
  tail_num:string{8} actual_elapsed_time:integer \
```

```
  crs_elapsed_time:integer air_time:integer arr_delay:integer \
  dep_delay:integer origin:string{3}:index dest:string{3}:index \
  distance:integer taxi_in:integer taxi_out:integer \
  cancelled:boolean:index cancellation_code:string{1} \
  diverted:boolean carrier_delay:integer weather_delay:integer \
  nas_delay:integer security_delay:integer \
  late_aircraft_delay:integer
```

Load the Data

This is a large data file, so we are going to optimize the load and use raw SQL instead of ActiveRecord to create these records.

Taking a note from Sandi Metz in *Practical Object-Oriented Design in Ruby* (POODR), I've abstracted out the data sanitation to a module. I put this in a file called `db_sanitize.rb` in the `lib` directory:

```
module DBSanitize
  def string(value)
    value.gsub!(/'/, '') unless value.nil?
    value.nil? ? 'NULL' : "'#{value}'"
  end
  def integer(value)
    value.nil? ? 'NULL' : Integer(value)
  end
  def boolean(value)
    value == '1'
  end
end
```

I like this a lot better. Note that this code is not automatically loaded, so you have to require the file before including it. I put this at the top of the rake file under the CSV `require` statement:

```
require 'db_sanitize'
include DBSanitize
```

Now we can sanitize (clean) our data as we read it. I tested bulk insert versus inserting one record at a time with this data. I was surprised to see that the bulk insert did not save any time. Here is the rake task to import the departure data:

```
CSV::Converters[:na_to_nil] = lambda do |field|
  field && field == "NA" ? nil : field
end
desc "Import flight departures data"
task :import_departures => :environment do
  if Departure.count == 0
    filename  = Rails.root.join('db', 'data_files', '1999.csv')
```

```
    timestamp = Time.now.to_s(:db)
    CSV.foreach(
      filename,
      :headers           => true,
      :header_converters => :symbol,
      :converters        => [:na_to_nil]
    ) do |row|
      puts "#{$.} #{Time.now}" if $. % 10000 == 0
      data = {
        :year                => integer(row[:year]),
        :month               => integer(row[:month]),
        :day_of_month        => integer(row[:dayofmonth]),
        :day_of_week         => integer(row[:dayofweek]),
        :dep_time            => integer(row[:deptime]),
        :crs_dep_time        => integer(row[:crsdeptime]),
        :arr_time            => integer(row[:arrtime]),
        :crs_arr_time        => integer(row[:crsarrtime]),
        :unique_carrier      => string(row[:uniquecarrier]),
        :flight_num          => integer(row[:flightnum]),
        :tail_num            => string(row[:tailnum]),
        :actual_elapsed_time => integer(row[:actualelapsedtime]),
        :crs_elapsed_time    => integer(row[:crselapsedtime]),
        :air_time            => integer(row[:airtime]),
        :arr_delay           => integer(row[:arrdelay]),
        :dep_delay           => integer(row[:depdelay]),
        :origin              => string(row[:origin]),
        :dest                => string(row[:dest]),
        :distance            => integer(row[:distance]),
        :taxi_in             => integer(row[:taxiin]),
        :taxi_out            => integer(row[:taxiout]),
        :cancelled           => boolean(row[:cancelled]),
        :cancellation_code   => string(row[:cancellationcode]),
        :diverted            => boolean(row[:diverted]),
        :carrier_delay       => integer(row[:carrierdelay]),
        :weather_delay       => integer(row[:weatherdelay]),
        :nas_delay           => integer(row[:nasdelay]),
        :security_delay      => integer(row[:securitydelay]),
        :late_aircraft_delay => integer(row[:lateaircraftdelay]),
        :created_at          => string(timestamp),
        :updated_at          => string(timestamp)
      }
      sql = "INSERT INTO departures (#{data.keys.join(',')})"
      sql += " VALUES (#{data.values.join(',')})"
      ActiveRecord::Base.connection.execute(sql)
    end
  end
end
```

Run the migration and rake task (`bundle exec rake db:migrate db:seed:import_departures`). The departures data took about a half hour to load on my computer. Maybe (hopefully) yours is faster than mine. Alternately I created a dump file using `pg_dump` that you can load a little quicker:

```
pg_restore -v -d departures_development -j3 db/data_files/departures.
        dump
```

I feel inclined to point out, as a matter of perspective, that these immense file loads are not something that you would do in production very often. In the "real world" you'd be accumulating these data gradually over time. In essence we are playing catch-up with those production apps.

Code Checkpoint

To see the code at this stage, go to https://github.com/DataVizToolkit/departures/tree/ch06.3.

Foreign Keys

Now that we have the data loaded there is one more thing I want to do with the `departures` table. We can use the Rails generator to create a migration (`rails g migration AddForeignKeysToDepartures`). Here are contents of the `change` method:

```
add_foreign_key :departures, :carriers, :column => :unique_carrier, :primary_key => :code
add_foreign_key :departures, :airports, :column => :origin, :primary_key => :iata
add_foreign_key :departures, :airports, :column => :dest, :primary_key => :iata
```

Why did we do this when we add the relationships in the models with `belongs_to` and `has_many`, you ask? Doing those things is definitely a good idea. However, neither of them are absolute safeguards. To truly enforce referential integrity, you have to actually enforce referential integrity. We could have done this before loading the data, but checking every record on insert makes data loads take a lot longer. Removing foreign keys and indexes for a large data load is a common strategy. Just remember to add them back!

Note

Referential integrity is the concept in a relational database where relationships among data (tables) should be enforced. It protects you from leaving orphaned records where you deleted the record that defines a foreign key's value.

The other thing to note is that the records for those foreign keys must already exist. That is why we loaded the airlines and carriers first.

Code Checkpoint

To see the code at this stage, go to https://github.com/DataVizToolkit/departures/tree/ch06.4.

Transforming the Data

Now that we have our data in place we can start asking questions of it and working through the matrix transformation.

Fetching the Data

Looking at all the departures for all of 1999 would not be very interesting. Carriers have different routes and different hubs, and there are a LOT of flights. The chord diagram would be a mess. Looking at departures for a given airline makes more sense.

Let's take a look at the origin/destination city pairs for American Airlines. The IATA code (abbreviation) for American Airlines is 'AA', Delta is 'DL', Southwest Airlines is 'WN', and so on. As a fun exercise later on, go back through and generate the chord diagrams for the other carriers in the data.

The following class method goes in the `Departure` class and begins the process of creating the matrix we need to feed the chord diagram:

```
def self.departure_matrix
  sql = <<-SQL.strip_heredoc
    SELECT origin, dest, count(*)
    FROM departures
    WHERE unique_carrier = 'AA'
    GROUP BY 1, 2
    ORDER BY 1, 2
  SQL
  counts = connection.execute(sql)
end
```

This query just gives us the counts. It does not generate a matrix for us. We need to take those counts and turn them into a matrix.

Generating the Matrix

Fortunately for us, Ruby has a `Matrix` class in the standard library. I'm not going to write this code directly in the `Departure` class, though. Create a module called `DepartureMatrix` (`app/models/departure_matrix.rb`).

```
require 'matrix'

module DepartureMatrix
  def airports_matrix!(counts:)
    h_matrix = counts.each_with_object({}) do |record, hash|
      hash[record["origin"]] ||= Hash.new(0)
      hash[record["origin"]][record["dest"]] = Integer(record["count"])
    end
    airports = h_matrix.keys.sort
    total    = Float(h_matrix.values.flat_map(&:values).sum)
    matrix   = Matrix.build(airports.count) do |row, column|
      origin = airports[row]
      dest   = airports[column]
      h_matrix.fetch(origin, {}).fetch(dest, 0) / total
    end
    [airports, matrix]
  end
end
```

The `airports_matrix!` method takes in a single parameter `counts`, which is what we just generated and returns a tuple (array with 2 items) with the list of airports and the matrix. We need both of these to tell D3 how to draw the chords and the labels.

There is a lot happening in this method, so let's walk through it.

```
h_matrix = counts.each_with_object({}) do |record, hash|
  hash[record["origin"]] ||= Hash.new(0)
  hash[record["origin"]][record["dest"]] = Integer(record["count"])
end
```

Enumerable is pretty amazing. Let's take a closer look at `Enumerable#each_with_object`. Here is a simplified example from the documentation:

```
evens = (1..10).each_with_object([]) { |item, array| array << item * 2 }
#=> [2, 4, 6, 8, 10, 12, 14, 16, 18, 20]
```

The `each_with_object` iterator takes a block that has two parameters. The first parameter is the item as we iterate through the collection. The second parameter is the object that we define in the parenthesis. In this case it is an array. In my code it is a hash.

The other tricky thing happening here is that I set a default value for each new origin hash. If there are missing values, they will be represented by the default value—zero in this case. The next thing we do is get a sorted list of airports. We can ask a hash for its keys, and what we get back is an array of keys. Pretty cool!

```
airports = h_matrix.keys.sort
```

Next we need to calculate the grand total of all the things. This is how we will know what percent each individual count represents. We just asked the hash for its keys, and now we are asking for its values.

```
total    = Float(h_matrix.values.flat_map(&:values).sum)
```

We have a multidimensional hash, so we get an array of arrays. We could `map` over those and flatten the resulting array, but `flat_map` gives us a nice shortcut for that combination of actions.

Do you remember significant digits from school? We need the total to be a float so that we don't lose the decimal point for downstream calculations.

```
matrix   = Matrix.build(airports.count) do |row, column|
  origin = airports[row]
  dest   = airports[column]
  h_matrix.fetch(origin, {}).fetch(dest, 0) / total
end
```

The final thing we need to do is actually generate the matrix. Here is a simple example of `Matrix#build` from the documentation:

```
m = Matrix.build(2, 4) {|row, col| col - row }
#=> Matrix[[0, 1, 2, 3], [-1, 0, 1, 2]]
```

The example builds a matrix with two rows and four columns. `Matrix#build` takes up to two parameters for the row and column counts. If you omit the second parameter, the column count will be set to the row count. I rely on that behavior in my code to generate a square matrix.

Finalizing the Matrix

Now that we have our matrix generator we need to put it to work. Go back to the `Departure` class and have it `extend DepartureMatrix`. Now `DepartureMatrix#airports_matrix!` becomes a class method in `Departure`. We just need to call it, like so:

```
def self.departure_matrix
  sql = <<-SQL.strip_heredoc
    SELECT origin, dest, count(*)
    FROM departures
    WHERE unique_carrier = 'AA'
    GROUP BY 1, 2
    ORDER BY 1, 2
```

```
  SQL
  counts = connection.execute(sql)
  airports_matrix!(:counts => counts)
end
```

You can run this from the console to see what your matrix looks like. It should be a large array of arrays.

Create the Views

We can turn our attention to creating the chord diagram now that we have our data in place. We need a controller, view, and routes to support the view and asynchronous data call.

Departures Controller and Routes

We need two routes and actions for the view and the AJAX data callback. Just as with the other apps and charts before, the index action does not need to do anything. The real work happens when the JavaScript function calls back to the server and asks for the data. Let's start by creating a controller (`rails g controller departures --skip-helper`). Put these actions in the `DeparturesController`.

```
  def index; end

  def departure_matrix
    airports, matrix = Departure.departure_matrix
    render :json => {
      :airports => airports,
      :matrix   => matrix
    }
  end
```

In order to make the controller actions do anything, we need to define some routes. Here is the cleaned up routes file:

```
Rails.application.routes.draw do
  root 'departures#index'
  get 'departures/index'
  get 'departures/departure_matrix'
end
```

Departures View

The view looks a lot like all the other views in this book. I pass the data route into the `makeChordChart()` function so we can use that it for multiple chord diagrams. This code goes in `app/views/departures/index.html.erb`:

```
<div id="chart"></div>

<script>
$(document).on('ready page:load', function(event) {
  // apply non-idempotent transformations to the body
  makeChordChart('/departures/departure_matrix.json');
});
</script>
```

We also need to include the D3 library in the application layout (`app/views/layouts/application.html.erb`). Put this before the application's JavaScript is loaded:

```
<%= javascript_include_tag
➥'https://cdnjs.cloudflare.com/ajax/libs/d3/3.5.17/d3.min.js' %>
```

Departures Style

The stylesheet looks very similar to the other stylesheets. Put this code in `app/assets/stylesheets/departures.scss`:

```
@import
➥url(http://fonts.googleapis.com/css?family=PT+Serif|PT+Serif:b|PT+Serif:
➥i|PT+Sans|PT+Sans:b);

body {
  background: #fcfcfa;
  color: #333;
  font-family: "PT Serif", serif;
  margin: 1em auto 4em auto;
  position: relative;
  width: 960px;
}

svg {
  font: 10px sans-serif;
}

#circle circle {
  fill: none;
  pointer-events: all;
}

.group path {
  fill-opacity: .5;
}

path.chord {
  stroke: #000;
  stroke-width: .25px;
```

```
}

#circle:hover path.fade {
  display: none;
}
```

Draw the Chord Diagram

One of my favorite visualizations is Mike Bostock's "Uber Rides by Neighborhood" chord diagram (https://bost.ocks.org/mike/uberdata/). This is a very good foundation for us for the task at hand. In fact, the main differences between my version and his are cosmetic. The JavaScript goes in `app/assets/javascripts/departures.js`.

Listing 6.1 Chord Diagram JavaScript

```
function makeChordChart(route) {
  var width         = 720,
      height        = 720,
      outerRadius   = Math.min(width, height) / 2 - 30,
      innerRadius   = outerRadius - 24
      formatPercent = d3.format(".1%"),
      color         = d3.scale.category20();

  var arc = d3.svg.arc()
      .innerRadius(innerRadius)
      .outerRadius(outerRadius);

  var layout = d3.layout.chord()
      .padding(.04)
      .sortSubgroups(d3.descending)
      .sortChords(d3.ascending);

  var path = d3.svg.chord()
      .radius(innerRadius);

  var svg = d3.select("#chart").append("svg")
      .attr("width", width)
      .attr("height", height)
    .append("g")
      .attr("id", "circle")
      .attr("transform", "translate(" + width / 2 + "," + height / 2 +
➥")");

  svg.append("circle")
      .attr("r", outerRadius);

  svg.append("text")
      .attr('class', 'chart_title')
```

```
      .attr("x", 0)
      .attr("y", -340)
      .attr("text-anchor", "middle")
      .style("font-size", "16px")
      .text("American Airlines City Pairs (1999)");

  d3.json(route, function(error, data) {
    var airports = data.airports;

    // Compute the chord layout.
    layout.matrix(data.matrix);

    // Add a group per origin.
    var group = svg.selectAll(".group")
        .data(layout.groups)
      .enter().append("g")
        .attr("class", "group")
        .on("mouseover", mouseover);

    // Add a mouseover title.
    group.append("title").text(function(d, i) {
      return airports[i] + ": " + formatPercent(d.value) + " of origins";
➥});

    // Add the group arc.
    var groupPath = group.append("path")
        .attr("id", function(d, i) { return "group" + i; })
        .attr("d", arc)
        .style("fill", function(d, i) { return color(i); });

    // Add a text label.
    var groupText = group.append("text")
        .attr("x", 6)
        .attr("dy", 15);

    groupText.append("textPath")
        .attr("xlink:href", function(d, i) { return "#group" + i; })
        .text(function(d, i) { return airports[i]; });

    // Remove the labels that don't fit. :(
    groupText.filter(function(d, i) { return
➥groupPath[0][i].getTotalLength() / 2 - 16 <
➥this.getComputedTextLength(); })
        .remove();

    // Add the chords.
    var chord = svg.selectAll(".chord")
        .data(layout.chords)
      .enter().append("path")
```

```
      .attr("class", "chord")
      .style("fill", function(d) { return color(d.source.index); })
      .attr("d", path);

    // Add an elaborate mouseover title for each chord.
    chord.append("title").text(function(d) {
      return airports[d.source.index]
          + " → " + airports[d.target.index]
          + ": " + formatPercent(d.source.value)
          + "\n" + airports[d.target.index]
          + " → " + airports[d.source.index]
          + ": " + formatPercent(d.target.value);
    });
    function mouseover(d, i) {
      chord.classed("fade", function(p) {
        return p.source.index != i
            && p.target.index != i;
      });
    }
  });
}
```

The title is hard-coded for American Airlines. If you do explore what the city pairs for other airlines look like consider a small refactor to allow for more generic JavaScript.

The chord diagram for American Airlines flights in 1999 can be seen in Figure 6.2. It may take a few seconds to pull the data and load in the browser.

Code Checkpoint

To see the code at this stage, go to https://github.com/DataVizToolkit/departures/tree/ch06.5.

Disjointed City Pairs

Airlines are very good at resource optimization. An airplane goes from airport to airport, picking up and delivering passengers at each stop. I wondered, though, how often does an airplane fly an "empty leg" route? By that I mean, how often is the destination airport different from the next origination airport for a given airplane? We have the data that we need to answer that question!

Using the Lead Window Function to Find Empty Leg Flights

The idea is simple enough. We have the airplanes' tail numbers, so we can track each plane's movements. We can ask Postgres to tell us the next origin airport using the LEAD window function and compare that to that record's destination airport. The

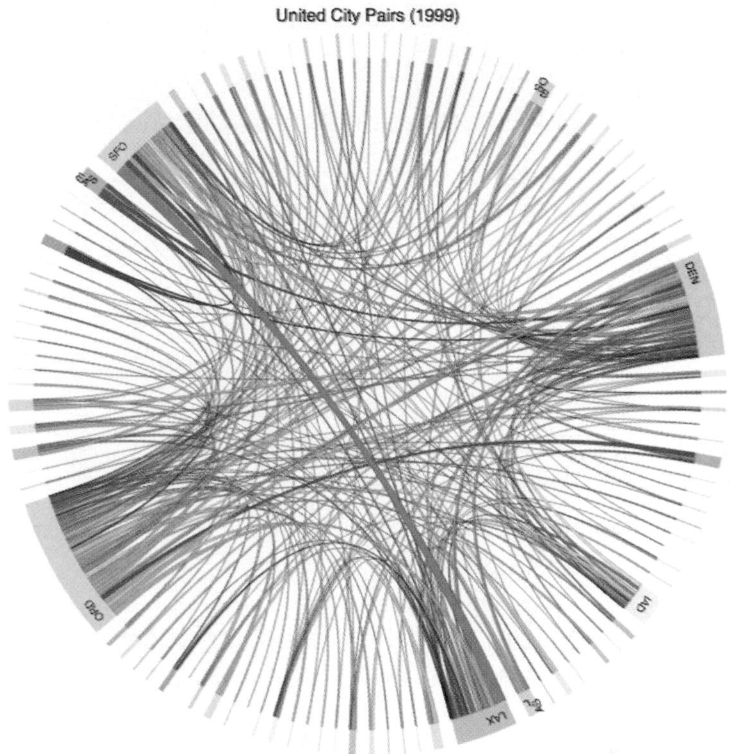

Figure 6.2 American Airlines Flights—1999

query to do all of those things requires a few steps, though. I typically use Common Table Expression (CTE) when I have queries with multiple parts that build on each other.

If you wanted to just write out the query and see the data, it would look like this:

```
WITH base_query AS (
  SELECT id,
    unique_carrier,
    flight_num,
    tail_num,
    origin,
    dest,
    to_date((((year || '-'::text) || month) || '-'::text) ||
➥day_of_month, 'YYYY-MM-DD'::text) AS dep_date,
    dep_time,
    arr_time,
    actual_elapsed_time,
```

```
    dep_delay,
    arr_delay,
    diverted
   FROM departures
   WHERE unique_carrier = 'AA'
), departures_with_lead AS (
  SELECT *,
    LEAD(origin) OVER (PARTITION BY tail_num ORDER BY tail_num, dep_date,
➥dep_time) AS next_origin
  FROM base_query
)
SELECT * FROM departures_with_lead
WHERE unique_carrier = 'AA'
  AND dest <> next_origin;
```

Go ahead and open your favorite SQL editor, or go into `rails dbconsole`, and run that query.

It's not crazy slow, but it's also not fast. For that reason, I will optimize and put the base query in a materialized view.

Optimizing Slow Queries with the Materialized View

A view is just a query that is stored in the database. A materialized view is where the query AND the results are stored in the database. You can index and update the data in a materialized view. We won't need to update this data, but indexes will be handy.

We can use Rails's migrations to do this for us. Create a migration (`rails g migration create_aa_departures`). Put the following code in the new migration and run the migration:

```
class CreateAaDepartures < ActiveRecord::Migration
  def up
    sql = <<-SQL.strip_heredoc
      CREATE MATERIALIZED VIEW aa_departures AS (
        WITH base_query AS (
          SELECT id,
            unique_carrier,
            flight_num,
            tail_num,
            origin,
            dest,
            to_date((((year || '-'::text) || month) || '-'::text) ||
➥day_of_month, 'YYYY-MM-DD'::text) AS dep_date,
            dep_time,
            arr_time,
            actual_elapsed_time,
            dep_delay,
            arr_delay,
```

```
            diverted
          FROM departures
          WHERE unique_carrier = 'AA'
      )
      SELECT *,
        LEAD(origin) OVER (PARTITION BY tail_num ORDER BY tail_num,
➥dep_date, dep_time) AS next_origin
      FROM base_query
    );
    CREATE INDEX ON aa_departures USING btree (origin);
    CREATE INDEX ON aa_departures USING btree (dest);
    CREATE INDEX ON aa_departures USING btree (next_origin);
  SQL
end

def down
  execute("DROP MATERIALIZED VIEW aa_departures;")
end
end
```

Draw the Disjointed City Pairs Chord Diagram

The query was the hard part. Now we just need to add the plumbing in the `DeparturesController` to query the data and serve it to the JavaScript.

The new controller methods should look very familiar:

```
def disjointed; end
def disjointed_matrix
  airports, matrix = Departure.disjointed_matrix
  render :json => {
    :airports => airports,
    :matrix   => matrix
  }
end
```

Don't forget to add routes for the `disjointed` and `disjointed_matrix` actions. The view `app/views/departures/disjointed.html.erb` is simply a copy of `index.html.erb` with the route changed for the data call:

```
makeChordChart('/departures/disjointed_matrix.json');
```

Now for the `Departure` model. You've seen the full query, and you saw how we broke it up to create the materialized view. We put the pieces back together in `Departure#disjointed_matrix`.

```
def self.disjointed_matrix
  sql = <<-SQL.strip_heredoc
```

```
    SELECT dest, next_origin, count(*)
    FROM aa_departures
    WHERE dest <> next_origin
      AND next_origin IS NOT NULL
    GROUP BY 1, 2
    ORDER BY 1, 2
  SQL
  counts = connection.execute(sql)
  airports_matrix!(:counts => counts, :field1 => "dest", :field2 => "next_origin")
end
```

You may have noticed that we now have three parameters in the `DepartureMatrix#airports_matrix!` call. We need to update that method. The modified code is below with the updated lines in bold.

```
def airports_matrix!(counts:, field1: "origin", field2: "dest")
  h_matrix = counts.each_with_object({}) do |record, hash|
    hash[record[field1]] ||= Hash.new(0)
    hash[record[field1]][record[field2]] = Integer(record["count"])
```

Figure 6.3 Disjointed City Pair Chord Chart

```
  end
  airports = h_matrix.keys.sort
  total    = Float(h_matrix.values.flat_map(&:values).sum)
  matrix   = Matrix.build(airports.count) do |row, column|
    origin = airports[row]
    dest   = airports[column]
    h_matrix.fetch(origin, {}).fetch(dest, 0) / total
  end
  [airports, matrix]
end
```

The field names in the queries are different, but the matrix creation routine is the same. We can simply pass in the data's hash key attributes, and everything still works.

You'll need to restart the Rails app if you still had it running because you've added new files. Go to http://localhost:3000/departures/disjointed and you should see a chord chart that looks like Figure 6.3.

Code Checkpoint

To see the code at this stage, go to https://github.com/DataVizToolkit/departures/tree/ch06.6.

Summary

In this chapter we created a new Rails app for flight departures. We loaded three new data files using both Ruby's CSV library and a custom import rake task. We learned about formatting options with Ruby's CSV library and also the Matrix class from Ruby's standard library. Finally, we drew two chord diagrams to look at the relationships between airports.

Chapter 7

Time Series Aggregates in Postgres

For the most part, every bit of your data has a timestamp. Each record (in a Rails app) probably has a timestamp for when it was created and when it was last updated. You may want to look at or analyze your data in uniform chunks of time. Maybe you want to look at hourly sales or daily rainfall, for example.

This chapter will walk you through how to split your data into uniform blocks of time, including time segments where there is no data. Armed with that information we will also draw a timeline using flight departure data from the previous chapter.

We will use this technique to answer the following question:

> What does an airplane's utilization look like?

Finding Flight Segments

The first thing we need to do to answer how often an airplane is used is find an airplane in the data. Let's take a look and see who flies their aircraft the most:

```
SELECT tail_num, unique_carrier, count(*)
FROM departures
WHERE tail_num <> 'UNKNOW'
GROUP BY 1, 2
ORDER BY 3 DESC
LIMIT 10;
```

Looking at the results you see that Southwest Airlines (WN) owns the top 10 (in this data from 1999):

```
 tail_num | unique_carrier | count
----------+----------------+-------
 N509     | WN             |  3313
 N513     | WN             |  3309
 N502     | WN             |  3287
 N514     | WN             |  3272
 N103     | WN             |  3271
 N501     | WN             |  3264
 N105     | WN             |  3259
 N82      | WN             |  3256
 N63      | WN             |  3256
 N510     | WN             |  3248
(10 rows)
```

Let's take a look at N509:

```
SELECT id, month, day_of_month, dep_time, arr_time,
  flight_num, origin, dest, distance
FROM departures
WHERE tail_num = 'N509'
ORDER BY year, month, day_of_month, dep_time
LIMIT 10;
   id    | month | day_of_month | dep_time | arr_time | flight_num |
➥origin | dest
---------+-------+--------------+----------+----------+------------+-----
➥---+------
 2042055 |     1 |            1 |      820 |      928 |        818 | SJC
➥| SNA
 2134606 |     1 |            1 |      955 |     1110 |        754 | SNA
➥| OAK
 2041051 |     1 |            1 |     1145 |     1259 |        841 | OAK
➥| SNA
 2027659 |     1 |            1 |     1315 |     1425 |        724 | SNA
➥| SJC
 2042206 |     1 |            1 |     1450 |     1600 |        868 | SJC
➥| SNA
 2134637 |     1 |            1 |     1620 |     1731 |        780 | SNA
➥| OAK
 2041020 |     1 |            1 |     1800 |     1915 |        836 | OAK
➥| SNA
 2027721 |     1 |            1 |     1935 |     2045 |        795 | SNA
➥| SJC
 2069352 |     1 |            1 |     2130 |     2233 |       1091 | SJC
➥| LAX
 1963698 |     1 |            2 |      700 |      905 |        603 | LAX
➥| PHX
(10 rows)
```

N509 flew nine times on January 1, 1999. Southwest Airlines specializes in short-haul flights, and you can see that in the data. The flights were all fairly short and in Southern California.

Creating a Series of Time

Postgres gives us the capability to create a series of values with the `generate_series` function. The documentation gives a handful of examples. Here is the simplest:

```
SELECT * FROM generate_series(2,4);
 generate_series
-----------------
               2
               3
               4
```

You can see that you get a series of values with one per row. We can use the `generate_series` function to generate hourly timestamps like this:

```
SELECT *
FROM generate_series(
    '1999-01-01 00:00'::timestamp,
    '1999-12-31 23:00'::timestamp,
    '1 hour') AS hourly;
       hourly
---------------------
 1999-01-01 00:00:00
 1999-01-01 01:00:00
 1999-01-01 02:00:00
[...and so on...]
```

Turning Data into Time Series Data

Now that you've seen the two building blocks of our time series data we need to put them together. We will use Common Table Expression (CTE) to define the auxiliary queries (subqueries) for the `generate_series` and the departures, and we will use a RIGHT JOIN to combine them. We do this so that we have at least one record for every time. The RIGHT JOIN enables us to have NULL values where the join does not find any records. See Chapter 5, "Window Functions, Subqueries, and Common Table Expression," for more on Common Table Expression and Appendix C, "SQL Join Overview, " for more on SQL joins.

There is just one problem. We don't have a common timestamp field to join on. We need to calculate one. Postgres is pretty smart with dates and converting strings to dates. I generally enter timestamps in queries like this `'19991225'` and Postgres understands how to convert to a timestamp—even without the explicit cast to a timestamp.

For the sake of clarity, we will cast from a string to a timestamp in the format `YYYYMMDD HH24MI` as follows:

```
SELECT '19991225 1430'::timestamp AS THEDATE;
       thedate
---------------------
 1999-12-25 14:30:00
(1 row)
```

For more information on Postgres Date/Time formatting, go to http://www.postgresql.org/docs/9.5/static/functions-formatting.html.

Now all we need to do is construct the date string from fields that we have in the data: `year`, `month`, `day_of_month`, and `dep_time`. We also need to zero-pad most of the fields so that they are all the correct length. To do that we use the `LPAD` function. Postgres uses a double pipe `||` to concatenate strings together. Generating the date string looks like this:

```
(year::text || LPAD(month::text, 2, '0') || LPAD(day_of_month::
➥text, 2, '0') || ' ' || LPAD(dep_time::text, 4, '0'))::
➥timestamp AS departure_time
```

We need to recast all the integer fields to text because LPAD is a string function. Put it all together, and it looks like this:

```
WITH hours AS (
  SELECT *
  FROM generate_series(
      '1999-01-01 00:00'::timestamp,
      '1999-12-31 23:00'::timestamp,
      '1 hour') AS hourly
), flights AS (
  SELECT id, year, month, day_of_month, dep_time, arr_time,
    (year::text || LPAD(month::text, 2, '0') || LPAD(day_of_month::text,
➥2, '0') || ' ' || LPAD(dep_time::text, 4, '0'))::timestamp AS
➥departure_time,
    (year::text || LPAD(month::text, 2, '0') || LPAD(day_of_month::text,
➥2, '0') || ' ' || LPAD(arr_time::text, 4, '0'))::timestamp AS
➥arrival_time,
    flight_num, actual_elapsed_time, origin, dest, distance, tail_num
  FROM departures
  WHERE tail_num = 'N509'
  ORDER BY year, month, day_of_month, dep_time
)
SELECT ROW_NUMBER() OVER (ORDER BY hourly) AS row_id, hourly, id,
```

```
  departure_time, arrival_time, dep_time, arr_time, flight_num,
  actual_elapsed_time, origin, dest, distance, COALESCE(tail_num, 'NA')
FROM flights
RIGHT JOIN hours ON tsrange(hours.hourly, hours.hourly + '1 hour') @>
➥departure_time
WHERE tsrange('1999-01-01 00:00'::timestamp,
➥'1999-01-01 23:59'::timestamp) @> hourly;
```

If you have not yet been exposed to Postgres's `tsrange` or `daterange` datatypes, you're probably wondering what in the world is going on there. You could just as easily write that last line as:

```
WHERE hourly BETWEEN '1999-01-01 00:00'::timestamp AND '1999-01-01
➥23:59'::timestamp.
```

I love the `tsrange` and its operators and have started using the timestamp range for start and end timestamps.

If you need to set a default value where there were no records, you can use the `COALESCE` function like I did with the tail number.

The results of the query look like this:

```
 row_id |        hourly        |   id    |    departure_time     |
➥arrival_time       | dep_time | arr_time | flight_num |
➥actual_elapsed_time | origin | dest | distance | coalesce
--------+---------------------+---------+---------------------+----------
➥-----------+----------+----------+------------+--------------------+---
➥-----+------+----------+----------
      1 | 1999-01-01 00:00:00 |       ¤ | ¤                   | ¤
➥|         ¤ |        ¤ |        ¤ |                   ¤ | ¤      | ¤
➥|        ¤ | NA
      2 | 1999-01-01 01:00:00 |       ¤ | ¤                   | ¤
➥|         ¤ |        ¤ |        ¤ |                   ¤ | ¤      | ¤
➥|        ¤ | NA
      3 | 1999-01-01 02:00:00 |       ¤ | ¤                   | ¤
➥|         ¤ |        ¤ |        ¤ |                   ¤ | ¤      | ¤
➥|        ¤ | NA
      4 | 1999-01-01 03:00:00 |       ¤ | ¤                   | ¤
➥|         ¤ |        ¤ |        ¤ |                   ¤ | ¤      | ¤
➥|        ¤ | NA
      5 | 1999-01-01 04:00:00 |       ¤ | ¤                   | ¤
➥|         ¤ |        ¤ |        ¤ |                   ¤ | ¤      | ¤
➥|        ¤ | NA
      6 | 1999-01-01 05:00:00 |       ¤ | ¤                   | ¤
➥|         ¤ |        ¤ |        ¤ |                   ¤ | ¤      | ¤
➥|        ¤ | NA
      7 | 1999-01-01 06:00:00 |       ¤ | ¤                   | ¤
➥|         ¤ |        ¤ |        ¤ |                   ¤ | ¤      | ¤
```

```
➥|          ¤ | NA
      8 | 1999-01-01 07:00:00 |          ¤ | ¤                     | ¤
➥|          ¤ |          ¤ |          ¤ |                     ¤ | ¤     | ¤
➥|          ¤ | NA
      9 | 1999-01-01 08:00:00 | 2042055 | 1999-01-01 08:20:00 | 1999-01-
➥01 09:28:00 |        820 |       928 |         818 |                   68 |
➥SJC     | SNA   |        342 | N509
     10 | 1999-01-01 09:00:00 | 2134606 | 1999-01-01 09:55:00 | 1999-01-
➥01 11:10:00 |        955 |      1110 |         754 |                   75 |
➥SNA     | OAK   |        371 | N509
     11 | 1999-01-01 10:00:00 |          ¤ | ¤                     | ¤
➥|          ¤ |          ¤ |          ¤ |                     ¤ | ¤     | ¤
➥|          ¤ | NA
     12 | 1999-01-01 11:00:00 | 2041051 | 1999-01-01 11:45:00 | 1999-01-
➥01 12:59:00 |       1145 |      1259 |         841 |                   74 |
➥OAK     | SNA   |        371 | N509
     13 | 1999-01-01 12:00:00 |          ¤ | ¤                     | ¤
➥|          ¤ |          ¤ |          ¤ |                     ¤ | ¤     | ¤
➥|          ¤ | NA
     14 | 1999-01-01 13:00:00 | 2027659 | 1999-01-01 13:15:00 | 1999-01-
➥01 14:25:00 |       1315 |      1425 |         724 |                   70 |
➥SNA     | SJC   |        342 | N509
     15 | 1999-01-01 14:00:00 | 2042206 | 1999-01-01 14:50:00 | 1999-01-
➥01 16:00:00 |       1450 |      1600 |         868 |                   70 |
➥SJC     | SNA   |        342 | N509
     16 | 1999-01-01 15:00:00 |          ¤ | ¤                     | ¤
➥|          ¤ |          ¤ |          ¤ |                     ¤ | ¤     | ¤
➥|          ¤ | NA
     17 | 1999-01-01 16:00:00 | 2134637 | 1999-01-01 16:20:00 | 1999-01-
➥01 17:31:00 |       1620 |      1731 |         780 |                   71 |
➥SNA     | OAK   |        371 | N509
     18 | 1999-01-01 17:00:00 |          ¤ | ¤                     | ¤
➥|          ¤ |          ¤ |          ¤ |                     ¤ | ¤     | ¤
➥|          ¤ | NA
     19 | 1999-01-01 18:00:00 | 2041020 | 1999-01-01 18:00:00 | 1999-01-
➥01 19:15:00 |       1800 |      1915 |         836 |                   75 |
➥OAK     | SNA   |        371 | N509
     20 | 1999-01-01 19:00:00 | 2027721 | 1999-01-01 19:35:00 | 1999-01-
➥01 20:45:00 |       1935 |      2045 |         795 |                   70 |
➥SNA     | SJC   |        342 | N509
     21 | 1999-01-01 20:00:00 |          ¤ | ¤                     | ¤
➥|          ¤ |          ¤ |          ¤ |                     ¤ | ¤     | ¤
➥|          ¤ | NA
     22 | 1999-01-01 21:00:00 | 2069352 | 1999-01-01 21:30:00 | 1999-01-
➥01 22:33:00 |       2130 |      2233 |        1091 |                   63 |
➥SJC     | LAX   |        308 | N509
     23 | 1999-01-01 22:00:00 |          ¤ | ¤                     | ¤
➥|          ¤ |          ¤ |          ¤ |                     ¤ | ¤     | ¤
```

```
➥|           ¤ | NA
     24 | 1999-01-01 23:00:00 |          ¤ | ¤                           | ¤
➥|           ¤ |           ¤ |           ¤ |                           ¤ | ¤       | ¤
➥|           ¤ | NA
(24 rows)
```

Graphing the Timeline

Running the time series query gives you a good perspective on the utilization of the aircraft. The results are a sort of text-based timeline. We can improve on that and make a graphical timeline.

Basic Timeline

You know the drill by now. We need to add routes, a view, and controller actions. Put these methods in `DepartureController`:

```
def timeline; end
def timeline_data
  data = Departure.timeline
  render :json => { :data => data }
end
```

We also need to execute the query. Take the query from the "Turning Data into Time Series Data" section above and put it in the `Departure` model:

```
def self.timeline
  sql = <<-SQL.strip_heredoc
    WITH hours AS (
      SELECT *
      FROM generate_series(
          '1999-01-01 00:00'::timestamp,
          '1999-12-31 23:00'::timestamp,
          '1 hour') AS hourly
    ), flights AS (
      SELECT id, year, month, day_of_month, dep_time, arr_time,
        (year::text || LPAD(month::text, 2, '0') ||
➥LPAD(day_of_month::text, 2, '0') || ' ' || LPAD(dep_time::text, 4,
➥'0'))::timestamp AS departure_time,
        (year::text || LPAD(month::text, 2, '0') ||
➥LPAD(day_of_month::text, 2, '0') || ' ' || LPAD(arr_time::text, 4,
➥'0'))::timestamp AS arrival_time,
        flight_num, actual_elapsed_time, origin, dest, distance, tail_num
      FROM departures
      WHERE tail_num = 'N509'
      ORDER BY year, month, day_of_month, dep_time
    )
    SELECT ROW_NUMBER() OVER (ORDER BY hourly) AS row_id, hourly, id,
```

```
      departure_time, arrival_time, dep_time, arr_time, flight_num,
      actual_elapsed_time, origin, dest, distance, tail_num
    FROM flights
    RIGHT JOIN hours ON tsrange(hours.hourly, hours.hourly + '1 hour') @>
➥departure_time
    WHERE tsrange('1999-01-01 00:00'::timestamp, '1999-01-01
➥23:59'::timestamp) @> hourly
  SQL
  counts = connection.execute(sql)
end
```

You can copy app/views/departures/index.html.erb to app/views/departures/timeline.html.erb and change the JavaScript function call to makeTimeline(). There is also a bit of SCSS style to add in app/assets/stylesheets/departures.scss:

```
// Timeline
.axis path, .axis line {
  fill: none;
  stroke: #000;
  shape-rendering: crispEdges;
}
path {
  fill: transparent;
  stroke: #000;
}
```

The trick to generating a timeline with D3 is that it's just an X-axis with timestamps as the ticks (see Listing 7.1).

Listing 7.1 Basic Timeline

```
function makeTimeline() {
  var margin = {top: 10, right: 0, bottom: 20, left: 0},
      width  = 960 - margin.left - margin.right,
      height = 300 - margin.top - margin.bottom;

  // Create a default datetime range for the axis
  var x = d3.time.scale.utc()
      .domain([new Date(1999, 0, 1), new Date(1999, 0, 2)])
      .range([0, width]);

  var xAxis = d3.svg.axis()
      .scale(x)
      .orient("bottom")
      .ticks(d3.time.hours)
      .tickSize(16, 0)
```

```
      .tickFormat(d3.time.format("%I %p"));

  var svg = d3.select("body").append("svg")
      .attr("width", width + margin.left + margin.right)
      .attr("height", height + margin.top + margin.bottom)
    .append("g")
      .attr("transform", "translate(" + margin.left + "," + margin.top +
➥")");

  svg.append("g")
      .attr("class", "x axis")
      .attr("transform", "translate(0," + height + ")")
      .call(xAxis)
    .selectAll(".tick text")
      .style("text-anchor", "start")
      .attr("x", 6)
      .attr("y", 6);

  d3.json('/departures/timeline_data?date=1999-01-01', function(error,
➥data) {
    var data = data.data;
    // reset the X axis to the correct day's hours
    var startDate = new Date(data[0].hourly);
    var endDate   = new Date(data[0].hourly);
    endDate.setDate(endDate.getDate() + 1);
    x.domain([startDate, endDate]);
    svg.select(".x.axis")
      .call(xAxis)
      .selectAll(".tick text")
        .style("text-anchor", "start")
        .attr("x", 6)
        .attr("y", 6);

    // Draw dots for the departures on the x-axis (timeline)
    svg.selectAll("dot")
        .data(data.filter(function(d) { return d.origin !== null }))
      .enter().append("circle")
        .attr("r", 3.5)
        .attr("cx", function(d) { return x(new Date(d.departure_time));
➥})
        .attr("cy", function(d) { return height; });
  });
}
```

We look at the utilization for a single day. In this example I have the date hard-coded for January 1, 1999. The code to generate the timeline is fairly simple because we are able to utilize D3's X-axis that already understands how to handle dates.

The timeline is simple, which can be a good thing. It's perhaps a little *too* simple, though. We can give the chart a bit more meaningful context by showing how long each flight is, and where each flight originated and landed.

Figure 7.1 presents the timeline.

Code Checkpoint

To see the code at this stage, go to https://github.com/DataVizToolkit/departures/tree/ch07.1.

Fancy Timeline

Taking the simple X-axis timeline that we just created, we can define a few more elements to give it more context. We define a function for drawing a curved line from the departure time to the arrival time. We also add some text to the timeline in the form of a chart title, plus a mouseover tooltip.

Listing 7.2 is the revised, full code with new sections noted in bold and with a double asterisk in the comments.

Listing 7.2 Fancy Timeline

```
function makeTimeline() {
  var margin = {top: 10, right: 0, bottom: 20, left: 0},
      width  = 960 - margin.left - margin.right,
      height = 300 - margin.top - margin.bottom;

  // Create a default datetime range for the axis
  var x = d3.time.scale.utc()
      .domain([new Date(1999, 0, 1), new Date(1999, 0, 2)])
      .range([0, width]);

  var xAxis = d3.svg.axis()
      .scale(x)
      .orient("bottom")
      .ticks(d3.time.hours)
      .tickSize(16, 0)
      .tickFormat(d3.time.format("%I %p"));

  // ** function to draw a curved line given 3 points
  var curved = d3.svg.line()
      .x(function(d) { return d.x; })
```

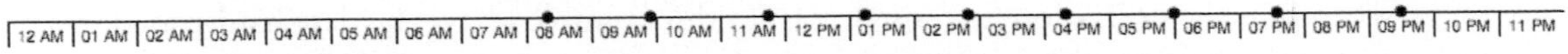

12 AM | 01 AM | 02 AM | 03 AM | 04 AM | 05 AM | 06 AM | 07 AM | 08 AM | 09 AM | 10 AM | 11 AM | 12 PM | 01 PM | 02 PM | 03 PM | 04 PM | 05 PM | 06 PM | 07 PM | 08 PM | 09 PM | 10 PM | 11 PM

Figure 7.1 Basic Timeline

```
        .y(function(d) { return d.y; })
        .interpolate("cardinal")
        .tension(0);

    var svg = d3.select("body").append("svg")
        .attr("width", width + margin.left + margin.right)
        .attr("height", height + margin.top + margin.bottom)
      .append("g")
        .attr("transform", "translate(" + margin.left + "," + margin.top +
➥")");

    svg.append("g")
        .attr("class", "x axis")
        .attr("transform", "translate(0," + height + ")")
        .call(xAxis)
      .selectAll(".tick text")
        .style("text-anchor", "start")
        .attr("x", 6)
        .attr("y", 6);

    // ** add a focus variable for mouseover tooltip
    var focus = svg.append("g")
        .attr("class", "focus")
        .style("display", "none");
    focus.append("text")
        .attr("x", 9)
        .attr("dy", ".35em");

    // ** Add a title to the chart
    svg.append("text")
        .attr('class', 'chart_title')
        .attr("x", width/2)
        .attr("y", height/2)
        .attr("text-anchor", "middle")
        .style("font-size", "16px")
        .text("Southwest Airlines Tail Number N509 (1999-01-01)");

    d3.json('/departures/timeline_data?date=1999-01-01', function(error,
➥data) {
      var data = data.data;
      var departures = data.filter(function(d) { return d.origin !== null
➥});
      // reset the X axis to the correct day's hours
      var startDate = new Date(data[0].hourly);
      var endDate   = new Date(data[0].hourly);
      endDate.setDate(endDate.getDate() + 1);
      x.domain([startDate, endDate]);
```

```
    svg.select(".x.axis")
      .call(xAxis)
      .selectAll(".tick text")
        .style("text-anchor", "start")
        .attr("x", 6)
        .attr("y", 6);

    // Draw dots for the departures on the x-axis (timeline)
    svg.selectAll("dot")
        .data(departures)
      .enter().append("circle")
        .attr("r", 3.5)
        .attr("cx", function(d) { return x(new Date(d.departure_time));
➥})
        .attr("cy", function(d) { return height; });

    // ** draw curved lines from the departure time to the arrival time
    var curve = svg.selectAll("curves")
        .data(departures)
      .enter().append("path")
        .attr("d", function(d) {
          var departureTime = new Date(d.departure_time);
          var middleTime    = new Date(d.departure_time);
          var arrivalTime   = new Date(d.arrival_time);
          middleTime.setMinutes(departureTime.getMinutes() +
➥+d.actual_elapsed_time/2)
          return curved([
            {x: x(departureTime), y: height},
            {x: x(middleTime), y: height - 15},
            {x: x(arrivalTime), y: height},
          ])
        })
        .on("mouseover", function() { focus.style("display", null); })
        .on("mouseout", function() { focus.style("display", "none"); })
        .on("mousemove", function(d) { mousemove(d) });

    // ** generate the text for the mouseover tooltip
    function mousemove(d) {
      var departureTime = new Date(d.departure_time);
      var x0            = x(departureTime);
      var y0            = height - 30;
      focus.attr("transform", "translate(" + x0 + "," + y0 + ")");
      focus.select("text").text(d.origin + " → " + d.dest);
    }
  });
}
```

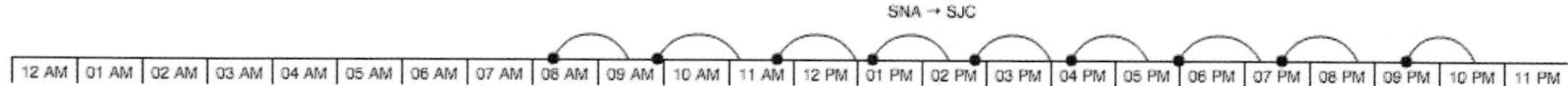

Figure 7.2 Fancy Timeline

The curved line is accomplished by drawing a third point between the departure time and the arrival time. The Y value for all the dots is the position of the timeline on the page. The curved line's midpoint Y value is set just a little higher up off the timeline. We set the interpolation to `cardinal`, which tells D3 to draw a curved line that hits all the points.

We call the `curved` function for each departure and pass in the array of three points for the line. There are some calculations that need to be done to figure the midpoint, so that attribute's function looks a little longer than usual.

Figure 7.2 presents the updated timeline.

Code Checkpoint

To see the code at this stage, go to https://github.com/DataVizToolkit/departures/tree/ch07.2.

Summary

In this chapter we dug a little deeper into the departures data to look at specific airplanes by tail number and how they are utilized. We used `to generate_series` to create a series of timestamps that we could join against the departures data to turn the individual departures for an airplane into time series data. We then created a simple timeline depicting each departure for Southwest Airlines tail number N509 on January 1, 1999. We then took that simple timeline and added curved lines to depict the departure and arrival times for each flight.

CHAPTER 8

Using a Separate Reporting Database

By now you've probably noticed that we sometimes jump through significant hoops to query the data we want for reporting purposes. Running reporting queries from your main application against your production (transactional) database can potentially take away from valuable resources. Imagine a report that takes more than a couple of seconds to run with an impatient user on the other side. *Click. Click. Click.* Before you know it you've tied up all available connections to the database and cannot conduct business until the connections clear.

Transactional versus Reporting Databases

What do I mean by "transactional" and why differentiate?

Simply put, your application exists to conduct transactions. They need not be credit card transactions or widget sales. Anything your users do that you store in the database is a transaction.

Generally speaking, your users don't really care about the metrics you're trying to keep an eye on. They don't even have access to them. Why should the queries that drive them take resources away from their experience on your site? If reports are a part of their workflow, like in the opening example, you need to think about how to isolate their footprint so they don't take away from the performance of your application in general.

Note

A transactional database's tables are usually normalized. That means the tables and their columns are organized to minimize data redundancy. Tables are linked together using foreign keys. Refer back to Chapter 6, "The Chord Diagram," for more on foreign keys.

The transactional database also needs to be able to read and write data quickly. Read/write optimization is beyond the scope of this book. I only bring it up to contrast it with a reporting database that is generally optimized for reads. The data in a reporting database is also denormalized. Each table is purpose-built to feed a reporting need. Data duplication is, therefore, not a concern in a reporting database.

Fortunately, there are a couple of ways that you can help isolate your reporting activities.

Worker Processes

Taking a step back from databases and reporting, one tactic is to take reports out of the request-response cycle. Put a job on a queue that can be picked up by a separate process from your main application. Rails has made this fairly easy to implement with ActiveJob (http://edgeguides.rubyonrails.org/active_job_basics.html).

Postgres Schemas

Background processes are fantastic. They won't be the answer to all of your problems, though (and they can create some of their own).

Rather than run a big query that transforms complex data on the fly to generate your metrics, you can transform the data in the background and put it in a new reporting database. Even better, Postgres schemas offer separate connections in the same database. Here is how the Postgres documentation explains schemas:

> A database contains one or more named schemas, which in turn contain tables. Schemas also contain other kinds of named objects, including data types, functions, and operators. The same object name can be used in different schemas without conflict; for example, both schema1 and myschema can contain tables named mytable. Unlike databases, schemas are not rigidly separated: a user can access objects in any of the schemas in the database he is connected to, if he has privileges to do so.

In other words, a database host has databases. A database has schemas. A schema has tables (and other objects). Access can be controlled to the databases as well as the schemas.

Working with Multiple Schemas in Rails

Getting your Rails app to talk to more than one database or schema is not hard, but there are a few things you need to do.

Defining the Schema Connection

The default schema is named `public`. You don't need to do anything to tell ActiveRecord to look in that schema for your tables. You can, however, tell ActiveRecord to look for tables and views in multiple schemas by adding a single line in the `database.yml` config file. Put this line in the `database.yml` file for the departures app where you define the username and password for the database connection.

```
schema_search_path: "public,reporting"
```

As long as the user has access to both schemas you are good to go now.

Creating a New Schema

We are just getting started. We've told ActiveRecord what to look for, but we haven't created the schema or put anything there to be found yet. We can do that with a migration (`rails g migration add_reporting_schema`):

```
class AddReportingSchema < ActiveRecord::Migration
  def up
    sql = <<-SQL
    CREATE SCHEMA IF NOT EXISTS reporting;
    GRANT ALL ON SCHEMA reporting TO postgres;
    SQL
    execute(sql)
  end

  def down
    sql = "DROP SCHEMA IF EXISTS reporting;"
    execute(sql)
  end
end
```

This will create the schema if it doesn't already exist. Your database user will have super user permissions in the new schema. The migration grants the postgres user access, which ensures that `pg_dump` and `pg_restore` will work. Those are the Postgres utilities to export and import data from the database. They're how you create a backup, and are also used when you run migrations to get the new schema file.

Speaking of the schema file, you need to change its format from Ruby to SQL. This enables us to have a more complicated database setup than what the Ruby schema file can communicate. Again, that's a simple single-line addition. This time the change is made in `config/application.rb`.

```
config.active_record.schema_format = :sql
```

With that in place you should be able to run the migration to get your new schema. If all goes well, you'll also get a new file called `db/structure.sql` with all the SQL required to create all of your database objects. You can delete `db/schema.rb` because it won't be used anymore.

Go ahead and run `bundle exec rake db:migrate` if you haven't already to create the new schema. If you run the migration and receive an error that role `postgres` does not exist, do the following.

1. Run `rails dbconsole`.
2. See what roles are specified in your database by running `SELECT * FROM pg_roles`.
3. Change the migration to one of the roles available to your user, and rerun it.

Code Checkpoint

To see the code at this stage, go to https://github.com/DataVizToolkit/departures/tree/ch08.1.

Creating Objects in the Reporting Schema

Now that we have a schema dedicated to reporting data and queries, we need to put some data there to be queried.

Materialized View in the Reporting Schema

We first used materialized views in Chapter 6, "The Chord Diagram." We embedded raw SQL in a migration to create the materialized view, but there is an alternative that helps clean up your code thanks to ThoughtBot and the Scenic gem (https://github.com/thoughtbot/scenic). The definition of a view (or materialized view) goes in a separate file. Add the Scenic gem to your Gemfile (`gem 'scenic'`) and run `bundle install`.

The Scenic Generator

Scenic gives us some new generators. The `scenic:model` generator will create a migration, model, test with fixture, and a file for the SQL statement.

```
rails generate scenic:model june_departure --materialized
```

We can tell Scenic to make the view a materialized view by passing in the `--materialized` flag. The materialized view will be called `june_departures`.

SQL Statement File

The first thing you need to do is rename the SQL statement file to include the schema in the name.

```
mv db/views/june_departures_v01.sql → db/views/reporting.june_departures
➥_v01.sql
```

The contents of the `reporting.june_departures_v01.sql` is just a query:

```
SELECT
  id,
  unique_carrier,
  flight_num,
  tail_num,
  origin,
  dest,
  LEAD(origin) OVER(PARTITION BY tail_num ORDER BY day_of_month,
➥dep_time) AS next_origin,
  to_date(year || '-' || month || '-' || day_of_month, 'YYYY-MM-DD') AS
➥dep_date,
  dep_time,
  arr_time,
  actual_elapsed_time,
  dep_delay,
  arr_delay,
  diverted
FROM departures
WHERE year = 1999
  AND month = 6
  AND cancelled = false;
```

Migration for a Materialized View in the Reporting Schema

The corresponding migration should look fairly familiar. We get a new macro called `create_view` that looks a lot like `create_table`. We have to help ActiveRecord out a little by putting the fully qualified name of the table (including schema) in quotes. Other than that, there is nothing out of the ordinary with this migration.

```
class CreateJuneDepartures < ActiveRecord::Migration
  def change
    create_view "reporting.june_departures", materialized: true
    add_index "reporting.june_departures", :tail_num
```

```
    add_index "reporting.june_departures", :origin
    add_index "reporting.june_departures", :dest
    add_index "reporting.june_departures", :unique_carrier
    add_index "reporting.june_departures", [:dep_date, :dep_time]
  end
end
```

The materialized view will be created (materialized) when you run the migration.

Model for a Materialized View in the Reporting Schema

The final thing is optional but a good idea. We can remind ActiveRecord that the table is in a different schema by providing the fully qualified name in the model. See the bold line in the following:

```
class JuneDeparture < ActiveRecord::Base
  # NOTE: if you do not specify this, the schema is still in the
  # search path, so ActiveRecord will still find the table.
  # Name collisions between schema would be a problem.
  self.table_name = "reporting.june_departures"
  def self.refresh
    Scenic.database.refresh_materialized_view(table_name)
  end
end
```

Accessing Data in the Reporting Schema

Now that we've done all of that we can query the data using ActiveRecord!

```
>> JuneDeparture.first
  JuneDeparture Load (8.5ms)  SELECT  "reporting"."june_departures".*
➥FROM "reporting"."june_departures" LIMIT 1
=> #<JuneDeparture id: nil, unique_carrier: "NW", flight_num: 570,
➥tail_num: "A367NW", origin: "MSP", dest: "MIA", next_origin: "MIA",
➥dep_date: "1999-06-01", dep_time: 738, arr_time: 1202,
➥actual_elapsed_time: 204, dep_delay: -2, arr_delay: -6, diverted: false>
```

Code Checkpoint

To see the code at this stage, go to https://github.com/DataVizToolkit/departures/tree/ch08.2.

Tables in the Reporting Schema

The materialized view is nice because it's easy to refresh the data, and you also can be a little lazy with the migration by not having to list out all the fields and their types like you would have to do when you create a new table. We were able to `SELECT * FROM june_departures` to get what we needed.

You may decide that what you really want is an actual table.

Migration for a Table in the Reporting Schema

This time the migration will be for a standard table. The only twist is that it's going to go in the reporting schema instead of the public schema. All we have to do is replace the `:ua_departures` symbol with a string containing the fully qualified table name (including schema) and list out all of the fields. Create the model and migration using the Rails model generator (`rails g model ua_departure`).

```
class CreateUaDepartures < ActiveRecord::Migration
  def change
    create_table 'reporting.ua_departures' do |t|
      t.string :unique_carrier, limit: 8
      t.integer :flight_num
      t.string :tail_num, limit: 8
      t.string :origin, limit: 3
      t.string :dest, limit: 3
      t.date :dep_date
      t.integer :dep_time
      t.integer :arr_time
      t.integer :actual_elapsed_time
      t.integer :dep_delay
      t.integer :arr_delay
      t.boolean :diverted
      t.string :next_origin, limit: 3

      t.timestamps null: false
    end
  end
end
```

When you run this migration you will get a new table in the reporting schema. Take a look at the `structure.sql` file to see how the table and all of its related objects are documented by Postgres.

Model for a Table in the Reporting Schema

We set the `table_name` to the fully qualified name including schema. It's not necessary, but it's a good breadcrumb to leave for future you.

```
class UaDeparture < ActiveRecord::Base
  self.table_name = "reporting.ua_departures"
end
```

Bulk Inserting Records in Batches

There were several hundred thousand United Airlines departures in 1999. We could try to insert them all at once, but that would be a Bad Idea. If successful it would take a long time. Chances are that it would fail because you would fill up the log on the database. I learned that lesson the hard way.

I spent most of this section trying to convince you that sometimes the database is the best place to do a lot of data processing. It is really good at what it does, after all. In some cases, Ruby is better. Ruby has much nicer control structures (e.g., loops). We can also make use of Ruby's `lambda` to define a query and use recursion to keep calling it. Create a new rake task using the Rails generator (`rails g task reporting`). See Listing 8.1 for the contents of the new rake task.

Ruby's Lambda

Blocks, procs, and lambdas can be confusing. In general, they are all what is called a closure, or a bit of code nestled into the code around it. The contents of the closure are not known directly by the code around it. The closure executes its code and returns the results. Closures are not unique to Ruby, either. Lots of languages have the construct of a closure.

The lambda is commonly thought of as an anonymous function. You do not declare the lambda like you do the typical Ruby method. Instead you assign the code to a variable. That variable can be called, and it will execute its code. A lambda can take arguments. One of the things that differentiates a lambda from a proc is that the lambda checks to make sure it gets the right number of arguments, where a proc does not.

You may be wondering at this point why not just define a method for the code in the lambda. The reason is that the lambda can be passed as an argument to a method. You will see this in action in Listing 8.1.

Listing 8.1 Safe Bulk Insert Rake Task

```
namespace :db do
  namespace :reporting do
    desc "Insert UA Departures into the reporting schema"
    task :insert_ua_departures => :environment do
      UPDATE_LIMIT = 250_000
      CONN         = ActiveRecord::Base.connection

      def timestamp
        Time.now.utc.iso8601
      end
      def batch(sql_lambda:, limit: UPDATE_LIMIT, offset: 0, count:
```

```
           0)
          sql = sql_lambda.call(limit,offset)
          if (cmd_tuples = CONN.execute(sql).cmd_tuples) > 0
            count += cmd_tuples
            if count % (UPDATE_LIMIT*10) == 0
              print "\n#{timestamp} records so far: #{count} "
            else
              print "."
            end
            batch(
              :sql_lambda => sql_lambda,
              :limit      => limit,
              :offset     => offset+=limit,
              :count      => count
            )
          else
            puts "\n#{timestamp} Total records: #{count}"
          end
        end

        sql = lambda do |limit, offset|
          <<-SQL
            WITH base_query AS (
              SELECT id,
                unique_carrier,
                flight_num,
                tail_num,
                origin,
                dest,
                to_date((((year || '-'::text) || month) || '-'::text) ||
➥day_of_month, 'YYYY-MM-DD'::text) AS dep_date,
                dep_time,
                arr_time,
                actual_elapsed_time,
                dep_delay,
                arr_delay,
                diverted,
                created_at,
                updated_at
               FROM departures
               WHERE unique_carrier = 'UA'
            ), ua_departures AS (
              SELECT *,
                lead(origin) OVER (PARTITION BY tail_num ORDER BY tail_num,
➥dep_date, dep_time) AS next_origin
              FROM base_query
            )
            INSERT INTO reporting.ua_departures
            SELECT id, unique_carrier, flight_num, tail_num,
```

```
            origin, dest, dep_date, dep_time, arr_time,
            actual_elapsed_time, dep_delay, arr_delay,
            diverted, next_origin, created_at, updated_at
          FROM ua_departures
          LIMIT #{limit} OFFSET #{offset};
        SQL
      end

      batch(:sql_lambda => sql)
    end
  end
end
```

Execute the rake task with `bundle exec rake db:reporting:insert_ua_departures`. When it completes you can check the data. Go into the Rails console and fetch the first record (`UaDeparture.first`). I get a record with the ID of 375 for flight from SFO to PHL.

The `batch` method is the workhorse of this rake task. We run the query and get back the number of rows affected (`cmd_tuples`). We make use of the `LIMIT` and `OFFSET` options to step our way through the data. When there are no rows affected we know we are done.

Code Checkpoint

To see the code at this stage, go to https://github.com/DataVizToolkit/departures/tree/ch08.3.

Summary

In this chapter we took a slight departure from generating visualizations to discuss how to feed your reporting needs without creating drag on your application and users. We accomplish this by separating the normal transactional data and the reporting data into separate database schemas. I then discussed using the scenic gem to maintain views and materialized views in the reporting schema. Finally, I discussed creating a table in the reporting schema and safely bulk-inserting data into the table.

Part III

Geospatial Rails

So far we've talked about querying data using ActiveRecord and also using raw SQL. We've done several different data visualizations using that data. Those visualizations utilized several different types of graphs. All the applications we built have an additional component that we have not yet addressed.

They all have location information.

This next section will discuss how to work with geospatial data in Rails. In Chapter 9, "Working with Geospatial Data in Rails," we discuss PostGIS, the Postgres GIS extension. We discuss geographic data types and how to make use of them in your Rails apps. You also learn how to import data, specifically a geospatial data format called a shapefile.

In Chapter 10, "Making Maps with Leaflet and Rails," we create maps in all three of the apps we've built so that we can visualize the geospatial data. Finally, in Chapter 11, "Querying Geospatial Data," we dig a little deeper into geospatial queries and compare spatial queries to their ActiveRecord counterparts.

Chapter 9
Working with Geospatial Data in Rails

A discussion of geospatial data and how to make it dance in Rails could very easily be a book all to its own. My intent with this section is not to cover all things GIS but instead to give you enough knowledge to be productive and explore the subject further. I am opening the door and inviting you to walk through into an amazing room full of incredible things.

GIS Primer

We begin our intro to geospatial data with a brief overview of some GIS concepts. This will give us the foundation for the work we will do toward the end of this chapter and in the final two chapters when we create maps and look at geospatial SQL queries.

It's (Longitude, Latitude) Not (Latitude, Longitude)

You probably learned about coordinates being (latitude, longitude), but that is not their correct order in the world of geospatial data. In GIS we generally refer to coordinates in X, Y-axis form. Longitude is the X-axis, and latitude is the Y-axis. For the most part, all GIS software will follow this pattern. It is important to confirm, though. It is especially important to confirm the order when you are working with a third party API that offers geospatial endpoints.

You may wonder why we typically speak of them in reverse, and why we learn it "backward." Perhaps it goes back to what we could measure. Latitude is easy to measure from a ship's deck with a sextant. Measuring longitude required something special. NASA JPL's Dr. Jeff Norris gave a fascinating keynote at RubyConf in 2015 that included the history of nautical positional measurements (https://www.youtube.com/watch?v=BZg75PlmzXI).

Decimal Degrees

Decimal degrees (DD) are a unit of measure. In fact, it is the unit of measure that you are accustomed to seeing for coordinates. The location for the Empire State building in DD is (-73.985664, 40.748441). More decimal numbers equate to a higher degree of precision. At a single decimal place, you can resolve objects at the city level. Three decimal places gets you to street-level scale, and six decimal places are necessary to be able to specify individual people.

Degrees, Minutes, Seconds (DMS)

Degrees, minutes, seconds (DMS) are an alternative to using decimal degrees.

There are 360 degrees in a circle. The earth is a globe with the equator being a circle that circumscribes it. There are therefore 360 longitude degrees. They're broken up into East and West at the Prime Meridian. Longitude ranges from 0° to 180° East and 0° to 180° West. The Prime Meridian is the zero point.

There are 180° of latitude. The equator is the zero point for latitude. As the rings go further North and further South the latitude degree gets larger. The North Pole is +90° N and the South Pole is –90° S.

The location for the Empire State Building in DMS is the following:

- Latitude: 40° 44' 54.3876'' N
- Longitude: 73° 59' 8.3904'' W

Datum

Think about how you describe where something is. Do you use a reference point? The book is on the shelf. My office is on this road at this intersection. The pass went 27 yards from the line of scrimmage. Those are all examples of where something is in relation to something else.

A datum is simply a reference used for spatial measurements. A reference point is set, and something's location is relative to that point. In North America there are three main datums used:

- NAD27—North American Datum of 1927
- NAD83—North American Datum of 1983
- WGS84—World Geodetic System of 1984

NAD27 and NAD83 are strictly for North America location. NAD27 uses a reference point on a ranch in Kansas. NAD83 uses 250,000 points as reference and is much more accurate. WGS84 covers the entire globe and is used by the U.S. Department of Defense. GPS was developed by the Department of Defense, and WGS84 is the default datum used for recreational and commercial GPS.

Map Projection

Imagine a globe with a map in stained glass and a light shining inside. You can see the image of the map projected on a nearby wall. A map projection describes how we take the spherical map and display it on a flat surface.

You've seen a map where the longitude and latitude lines are a perfectly square grid. You've also seen a map with cutouts and curved longitude and latitude lines. The latter had a lot less distortion than the former. These are different map projections. The different map projections can distort the globe differently.

Spatial Reference System Identifier (SRID)

The Spatial Reference System Identifier (SRID) helps define how we calculate where, exactly, to place a given coordinate on the flat plane and how to calculate distances between coordinates. If you want to be very specific for a small section of geography, then you should use an SRID for that geography. For example, EPSG:2248 (http://spatialreference.org/ref/epsg/2248) is the projection for Maryland. The SRID would be 2248, and you could calculate very accurate distances within Maryland. Texas is large enough that it is split into five SRIDs (2275-2279).

On the other hand, if you wanted to be less specific, the default projection is EPSG:4326 (http://spatialreference.org/ref/epsg/4326). The SRID for this one is 4326, and if you do not specify one, this is usually what is assumed. This is also known as WGS84, described in the previous section.

Not to be outdone, Google has their own projection for Google Maps. Fortunately, all the major GIS packages know how to handle SRID 900913.

For the most part, you'll probably spend the vast majority of your time in good old 4326. When you work with oil and gas geographic data or data from local governments is when you start to get into the other, more specific, projections.

Three Feature Types

We will want to put things on our maps. These things are called features, and there are three types of features: point, line, and polygon. We can draw anything we need to draw with these three feature types.

Point

The simplest feature is a point (X, Y). Remember from "It's (Longitude, Latitude) Not (Latitude, Longitude)" that the X-axis is longitude, so a point is (longitude, latitude). Your phone's last known location is a point. If you have an application that stores location data be prepared for lots of writes and lots of records because it can accumulate quickly.

Line

A line (also known as linestring or polyline) is a sequence of points. Lines can curve. When you ask for directions from Google Maps (or whichever map app you prefer), you are shown a linestring for the route.

You can also have a multiline. As you may have guessed, there are multiple lines in that feature. The Great Wall of China could be an example of a multiline because it is considered a single feature but is actually comprised of several disconnected segments.

Polygon

Polygons have at least three sides and must be closed, otherwise it's just a line. The border of your city would be represented by a polygon.

Similar to the multiline, you can also have a multipolygon. The state of Kentucky could be a stored as a multipolygon. There is a disconnected piece of Kentucky called Kentucky Bend that is surrounded by Tennessee and Missouri. This geographic feature is known as an exclave.

PostGIS

PostGIS is a spatial database extender for Postgres. It adds support for geographic objects and enables location (spatial) queries to be run in SQL.

I mentioned in the intro for this section that all of our apps have location data. That's not actually true, yet. Two of the apps have longitude and latitude information. The Maryland residential sales app has a list of zip codes but no geographic information for those zip codes. Not to worry, though, we will address that.

Simply having a latitude and longitude is not enough to make our database understand them as a location coordinate. We need to teach Postgres how to handle GIS data specifically. For that we turn to the PostGIS extension.

Postgres Contrib Modules

Postgres is extendable. You can add to the core functionality with additional modules. Postgres ships with dozens of modules that are not part of the core system but can easily be used without having to install more software. If you've use the `hstore` datatype, then you've used one of these contrib modules. Most GUI tools (pgAdmin, for example) use the adminpack contrib module.

PostGIS does not ship with Postgres and does require some installation. The dependencies and installation process vary by system, but the core dependencies are:

`GEOS` - Geometry engine for GIS

`GDAL` - Geospatial Data Abstraction Library

`ProJ4` - Cartographic projection library

Installing PostGIS

As with most software, there are multiple ways to install PostGIS. You can do it manually and compile everything. I am actually not going to go over that option, though. There is an easier way to install PostGIS from the command line. Also, you may not need to install PostGIS, and I will discuss that as well.

The Manual Way

The easiest way to install PostGIS is with your system's package management system (homebrew, yum, or apt). These will generally handle all the dependencies as well. The installation instructions can be found at: http://trac.osgeo.org/postgis/wiki/UsersWikiInstall. .

The No-Install-Required Way

Don't start downloading and installing packages quite yet because you may already have PostGIS installed in your environment. If you use Postgres.app on OSX, you already have PostGIS. Heroku and Amazon RDS both support PostGIS without needing any further installation. There may be others as well.

To see if your database has support for PostGIS you can run this command:

```
SELECT name, default_version,installed_version
FROM pg_available_extensions
WHERE name LIKE 'postgis%';
```

You should see at least one record:

```
          name          | default_version | installed_version
------------------------+-----------------+-------------------
 postgis                | 2.2.1           | 2.2.1
```

PostGIS Functions

PostGIS has a lot of functions. You can see the subset of the list "which a user of PostGIS is likely to need" in the PostGIS reference (http://postgis.net/docs/reference.html).

The functions that I use the most tend to center around distance and whether something is within a geometry. We cover PostGIS functions in more detail in Chapter 11, "Querying Geospatial Data," but here is a quick overview to give you a taste of the sorts of things we can do in PostGIS.

ST_GeomFromText

Databases and languages have data types. GIS also has data types. The geometry data type is the basis for most, if not all, the GIS calculations you'll do. There are a lot of constructors that convert one form of input to a geometry. `ST_GeomFromText` is how you convert from a point, polygon, or line to a geometry.

ST_Centroid

The central point of a polygon is called the centroid. Similarly, the geometric center of a geometry is called the centroid. For lack of better information, I will use the centroid of a place to calculate distance from a point to that place.

ST_Distance versus ST_DistanceSphere

Calculating distance requires that you make a choice. The more accurate calculation is `ST_DistanceSphere` because it takes a spherical Earth into account. The `ST_Distance` calculation essentially assumes a flat Earth. While we know that the Earth is not flat, there are some scenarios where a flat Earth view is feasible or preferred. For example, flight simulators may use flat Earth projections and calculations.

Here is an example that calculates the distance from the centroid of a place to a point:

```
SELECT round(CAST(ST_DistanceSphere(ST_Centroid(the_geom),
➥ST_GeomFromText('POINT(-73.985664 40.748441)',4326)) AS numeric),2) AS
➥dist_meters
```

You see how much is packed into such a simple task. Once you get the hang of casting to a geometry datatype, and working with the right units, it flows a lot more naturally.

ActiveRecord and PostGIS

I've given you a high-level overview of the GIS concepts you'll see most often. Now it's time to turn our focus to Rails and integrating PostGIS into a Rails app.

ActiveRecord PostGIS Adapter

Configuring a Rails app to utilize PostGIS is remarkably simple. I'll get into the specifics in the next section. With the addition of the `activerecord-postgis-adapter` gem to your Gemfile, ActiveRecord can begin utilizing PostGIS functions. Take a look at the gem's documentation for more information (https://github.com/rgeo/activerecord-postgis-adapter).

Go ahead and include the gem in the departures app Gemfile and run `bundle install`.

Rails PostGIS Configuration

Once you've installed the `activerecord-postgis-adapter` gem you need to modify one more file. Open the `database.yml` file. We need to change the database adapter from `postgresql` to `postgis`.

Now add the PostGIS extension to the `departures_development` database with this rake task:

```
bundle exec rake db:gis:setup
```

Just having the extension available on the database server is not enough. You have to add the extension to each app's database specifically. This installs the geospatial functions in the database.

And with that in place you are ready to start playing with PostGIS!

Code Checkpoint

To see the code at this stage, go to https://github.com/DataVizToolkit/departures/tree/ch09.1.

PostGIS Hosting Considerations

I prefer to not set up production database servers from scratch. Configuring and tuning a database is not my strength. Heroku's Postgres and Amazon's RDS Postgres services are both very good and easy to use. If you use a different hosted PostgreSQL service, you should check to see if PostGIS is offered. If you're rolling your own server, then refer to the install instructions from earlier in this chapter.

Using Geospatial Data in Rails

The flight departures app's database is configured for PostGIS, but we have not configured any of the models or tables to have any of the GIS feature types yet. Let's update the flights model to include a `POINT`.

Creating Geospatial Table Fields

We can create GIS feature fields in our migrations thanks to the ActiveRecord PostGIS adapter. Use the Rails generator to create the migration (`rails g migration add_lon_lat_to_airports`). The migration to add a `POINT` to the `airports` table looks like this:

```
class AddLonLatToAirports < ActiveRecord::Migration
  def change
    add_column :airports, :lonlat, :st_point, :geographic => true
    add_index :airports, :lonlat, :using => :gist
  end
end
```

This gives us a point datatype called `lonlat` that we also told Postgres to index. You can look at the ActiveRecord PostGIS adapter documentation to see all of the field types that are supported. Don't forget to run the migration (`bundle exec rake db:migrate`).

Latitude and Longitude

I try to use ActiveRecord callbacks sparingly. They can get out of hand quickly. However, they are useful for filling in data when creating records and storing calculated data like a geometry. Bear in mind that we can also define default values for fields in our migrations.

Imagine a model where there are fields for longitude and latitude. In order to generate the `POINT` for each record as we load the data, we would simply need to add this to the `Airport` model:

```
module Factories
  GEO = RGeo::Geographic.spherical_factory(:srid => 4326)
end

before_create :set_lonlat

private
def set_lonlat
  self.lonlat = Factories::GEO.point(longitude, latitude)
end
```

This is how we tell RGeo, which the ActiveRecord PostGIS adapter sits on top of, how the data is projected.

We don't really need to imagine this model with longitude and latitude, though, because our `airports` table fits the bill. Using the code above as our template, we can update the `Airport` model to look like this:

```
class Airport < ActiveRecord::Base
  module Factories
    GEO = RGeo::Geographic.spherical_factory(:srid => 4326)
  end
  before_create :set_lonlat

  def longitude
    long
  end
  def latitude
    lat
  end
  def lonlat
    Factories::GEO.point(longitude, latitude)
  end

  private
  def set_lonlat
    self.lonlat = Factories::GEO.point(longitude, latitude)
  end
end
```

I added two convenience methods to provide attributes called `latitude` and `longitude` because that's what I would expect the fields to be called. The plumbing is also in place to create the `lonlat POINT` for each new record. Note that we have already loaded this table, so no records will currently have the `lonlat` set. I provided a helper method to calculate the value for **new** records. We can create a migration to fix the existing records. Hold that thought, we will come back to it.

Simple GIS Calculation

Rails knows how to calculate the distance between two airports now. We could see how far apart SFO in San Francisco and LGA in New York City are:

```
sfo = Airport.find_by(:iata => "SFO")
lga = Airport.find_by(:iata => "LGA")
distance_meters = sfo.lonlat.distance(lga.lonlat)
distance_miles = distance_meters * 0.000621371
=> 2575.9719632552024
```

Using the PostGIS functions in a query would look like this:

```
SELECT ST_DistanceSphere(
  ST_GeomFromText('POINT(-122.3748433 37.61900194)',4326), -- SFO
  ST_GeomFromText('POINT(-73.87260917 40.77724306)',4326)  -- LGA
)::NUMERIC * 0.000621371 AS dist_miles
```

Working with Shapefiles

A shapefile is a special file format to communicate geospatial information. It is actually a set of files that work together. The standard comes to us from Esri and can be used in PostGIS as well as other GIS viewers like ArcGIS.

Let's grab an airport's shapefile from https://catalog.data.gov/dataset/usgs-small-scale-dataset-airports-of-the-united-states-201207-shapefile. I put mine in the `tmp` directory in the departures app. You can also download the file on the command line:

```
curl -o tmp/airportx010g.shp.tgz http://dds.cr.usgs.gov/pub/data/
➥nationalatlas/airprtx010g.shp_nt00822.tar.gz
cd tmp
tar xzvf airportx010g.shp.tgz
rm airportx010g.shp.tgz
```

Shapefile Import Schema

While we are at it, let's also create a new schema in the `departures_development` database. We are going to do this manually using SQL. You can open up a GUI application, like pgAdmin, or log into the database from the command line using the `rails dbconsole` command.

Once you are at a SQL prompt you can create a new database schema with this SQL:

```
CREATE SCHEMA shapefiles
      AUTHORIZATION barrettclark; -- substitute your database username
```

Importing from a Shapefile

Now we have everything we need to import our shapefile and see the data. Unzip the zipped shapefile that you downloaded. You should see the following files:

airprtx010g.shp.dbf

airprtx010g.shp.prj

airprtx010g.shp.sbn

airprtx010g.shp.sbx

airprtx010g.shp.shp

airprtx010g.shp.shx

airprtx010g.shp.txt

airprtx010g.shp.xml

The command to import a shapefile is `shp2pgsql` (shapefile to pgsql). This will take all the data in the files above and translate them into SQL statements. You can either save the interim SQL statements in a file, or pipe them directly into `psql`. I'm going to do the latter, but I encourage you to experiment and see what the generated SQL looks like.

The full shapefile import looks like this:

```
shp2pgsql -s 4326 tmp/airprtx010g.shp.shp shapefiles.airports | psql -h
➥localhost -d departures_development -U barrettclark
```

Again, you would substitute your database user's username for mine.

Putting this into a new schema that isn't noted in the `database.yml` file means that it's outside the view of the Rails app. You won't see this schema or this table in the schema dump. It is visible within the Postgres server, though. You could reference the table in a query by including the schema with the table name (`shapefiles.airports`). This would come in handy in an import scenario where you need to do an ETL from a shapefile, and maybe you need to do some additional processing on the data before it goes into your desired database.

Shapefile ETL

I have worked in the travel industry for a few years, and I have never seen two airport lists have the same airports. Let's see how well the airports that we just imported from the shapefile line up with the airports we already have. To do that we will need a query that does a `RIGHT OUTER JOIN`. If you need to brush up on your SQL joins take a look at Appendix C, "SQL Join Overview."

The query to see all of the airports from both tables looks like this:

```
SELECT a1.iata, a1.state, a2.iata, a2.state
FROM airports a1
RIGHT OUTER JOIN shapefiles.airports a2 on a1.iata = a2.iata
  WHERE a2.iata <> 'NONE' AND cntl_twr = 'Y'
ORDER BY a1.iata, a2.iata;
```

Run that query in your favorite SQL editor, and you will see that there are some airports that we did not have in our existing airports table. We want those airports. We need those airports. We will have those airports.

We can `INSERT` the new airports, but starting in Postgres 9.5 we also gained the ability to update existing records in the same query. That's right, we are going to do an `UPSERT`! We can do this in a migration, too. Use the Rails migration generator to create a migration (`rails g migration airports_upsert`). We will configure this migration to not be reversible because once we update the data there is no way to undo it.

Listing 9.1 Airport **UPSERT** Migration

```
class AirportsUpsert < ActiveRecord::Migration
  def up
    sql = <<-SQL.strip_heredoc
      -- Begin by defining the airports from the shapefile that we
➥might want to insert
      WITH shapefile_airports AS (
        SELECT iata, airpt_name, city, state, 'USA',
          latitude, longitude, NOW(), NOW()
        FROM shapefiles.airports
        WHERE iata <> 'NONE' AND cntl_twr = 'Y'
      )
      -- INSERT INTO SELECT FROM query
      INSERT INTO airports (
        iata, airport, city, state, country,
        lat, long, created_at, updated_at
      )
      SELECT * FROM shapefile_airports
      -- UPSERT!!
      ON CONFLICT (iata) DO UPDATE SET
        lat=EXCLUDED.lat,
        long=EXCLUDED.long,
        updated_at=NOW();
    SQL
    connection.execute(sql)
  end

  def down
    raise ActiveRecord::IrreversibleMigration
  end
end
```

I begin the query by defining a subquery, in CTE form, to give us the full list of airports from the shapefile that we might want to insert. Look back at Chapter 5, "Window Functions, Subqueries, and Common Table Expression," to brush up on Common Table Expression (CTE).

The second phase is your standard `INSERT INTO` query where you `SELECT FROM` a table, or in this case, the CTE. It does not exclude records that already exist because we are taking advantage of the `UPSERT` functionality in the final phase of the query.

The final phase is the `UPSERT`, and it will only work on Postgres 9.5 and above. For any record that already has a matching `iata` value, we will update three fields.

The values from the shapefile record are put into an EXCLUDED record that we can tap into. We will grab the latitude and longitude from the shapefile airport, and we will also update the updated_at field to indicate when the record was updated.

If you have an older version of Postgres you will need to run the version of the SQL in Listing 9.2.

Listing 9.2 Alternate Airport **UPDATE** SQL

```
-- Begin by defining the airports from the shapefile that we might
➥want to insert
WITH shapefile_airports AS (
  SELECT iata, airpt_name, city, state, 'USA',
    latitude, longitude, NOW(), NOW()
  FROM shapefiles.airports
  WHERE iata <> 'NONE' AND cntl_twr = 'Y'
)
-- INSERT INTO SELECT FROM query
INSERT INTO airports (
  iata, airport, city, state, country,
  lat, long, created_at, updated_at
)
(
  SELECT * FROM shapefile_airports
  -- Filter for records that already exist
  WHERE NOT EXISTS (
    SELECT 1
    FROM airports
    WHERE airports.iata = shapefile_airports.iata
  )
)
```

After running the migration we can confirm that the UPSERT worked by looking at how many records were updated:

```
# SELECT COUNT(*) FROM airports WHERE created_at <> updated_at;
 count
-------
   431
(1 row)
```

Update Missing **lonlat** Data

It is time to come back to the lonlat field and fill in the data for the existing records. We do this with a simple migration that executes an UPDATE query. Since we cannot undo the update once it runs this migration is also not a reversible migration. The contents of the migration are:

```
class UpdateAirportLonLat < ActiveRecord::Migration
  def up
    sql = <<-SQL.strip_heredoc
      UPDATE airports
      SET lonlat = ST_GeomFromText('POINT(' || long || ' ' || lat ||
➥')',4326)
      WHERE lonlat IS NULL;
    SQL
    connection.execute(sql)
  end

  def down
    raise ActiveRecord::IrreversibleMigration
  end
end
```

Now we have all the airports, and we got to use some fairly new Postgres functionality.

Code Checkpoint

To see the code at this stage, go to https://github.com/DataVizToolkit/departures/tree/ch09.2.

Summary

We covered a lot of ground quickly in this chapter. Like I said in the beginning, this was not meant to be deep coverage of these topics. I wanted to give you some key highlights of general GIS concepts so that you could begin to play with them.

With the general foundation set, we went through some key aspects of PostGIS: what is it, how do you get it, and what can you do with it. You saw some strange function names, such as `ST_Distance`, and then you saw how to use them.

We incorporated PostGIS into a Rails app with just a few simple tweaks. Thanks to the hard work that has gone into the ActiveRecord PostGIS adapter, it is as simple as adding a gem and changing the database adapter name!

Finally, we loaded geographic data into the app's database by importing a shapefile. You could have also loaded a file like we did in previous chapters, and used the callback in the `Airport` model to handle the geography.

Chapter 10

Making Maps with Leaflet and Rails

In this chapter you learn about creating maps using a JavaScript library called Leaflet. We update all three of the apps that we have built throughout the book.

We begin learning about mapping with Leaflet by updating the weather app to show the location of all the weather stations that reported temperature in 1836.

Next we map the location of all the airports in California and implement a clustering strategy to visually simplify areas with high concentrations of airports. Once we've mapped the airports we will draw a flight path between two airports at opposite ends of the state.

Finally, we update the Maryland residential sales app by importing a shapefile for the zip codes so that we can map them. Then we transform the map into a choropleth by adding color to indicate the median value.

Leaflet

Leaflet is a JavaScript library for creating maps. It defines the functionality for drawing geographic elements on a web page using Scalable Vector Graphics (SVG). Leaflet has no dependencies and can be used in conjunction with popular libraries such as D3 and jQuery. Leaflet also has plug-ins for additional functionality or easier interaction with map content providers. We will use a handful of plug-ins from Mapbox.

Map Tiles

Leaflet does a lot of cool stuff, but you can't see any of it without some map imagery. You don't just get a giant image of a map to pan and zoom on, though. You get several sections of the map that Leaflet stitches together seamlessly to make the full

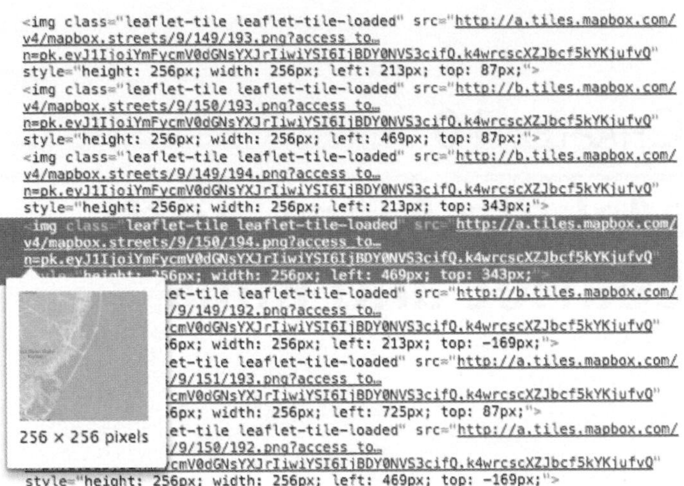

Figure 10.1 Rendered Map Tiles

map. These sections are called tiles. You can see an example of what these tiles look like in Figure 10.1.

Fresh tiles are served as you pan around. You also get a new set of tiles when you zoom in or out. Each zoom level has its own set of map tile imagery. Leaflet handles fetching the tiles and placing them on the page. The way that GIS software can seamlessly translate map projections and put them together still amazes me.

Map Layers

A map layer is a way to organize content in your map. The tiles from the previous section that are stitched together are usually called the base layer. This is generally the map without additional features added to it. It could be satellite view, terrain view, or whatever else the provider offers.

You can add layers on top of the base layer with various features or groupings of features (e.g., roads, traffic, points of interest). A map could have dozens of layers. Each layer's background is transparent so they do not interfere with each other. You can also add controls to your map that enable someone to turn layers on and off.

Leaflet does not provide a base layer for you but can be used with many different map tile providers. I'll be using Mapbox via the Mapbox Leaflet plug-in in this chapter. Other providers include Bing, Google, and OpenStreetMap. You can also run your own tile server.

Incorporating Leaflet into Rails to Visualize Weather Stations

Our first map will be a very simple one. The weather app's database is not set up for PostGIS and does not need to be. Everything we need to do is in the front-end.

Using a Separate Rails Layout for the Map

The first thing we need to do is create a new layout. The application layout in all of our apps includes the JavaScript tag to fetch D3 from its CDN. Leaflet is separate from D3, and we are not using the two of them together.

Making a new layout is as simple as copying the application layout to another file and then editing that new file. I called my new layout `map.html.erb`, and it looks like this:

```
<!DOCTYPE html>
<html>
<head>
  <title>NOAA Weather Data</title>
  <%= stylesheet_link_tag    'application', media: 'all', 'data-
➥turbolinks-track' => true %>
  <%= javascript_include_tag
➥"https://api.tiles.mapbox.com/mapbox.js/v2.2.4/mapbox.js" %>
  <%= stylesheet_link_tag
➥"https://api.tiles.mapbox.com/mapbox.js/v2.2.4/mapbox.css" %>
  <%= javascript_include_tag 'application', 'data-turbolinks-track' =>
➥true %>
  <%= csrf_meta_tags %>
</head>
<body data-mapbox-token="<%= ENV['MAPBOX_TOKEN'] %>">

<%= yield %>

</body>
</html>
```

The main difference is that the D3 references are removed and two new references to Mapbox are included. You'll also notice the additional data stored in the body tag. We will have an API token for Mapbox that we do not want to have exposed in our code or in our JavaScript. We can tap into environment variables like we would for other services, but getting them into the JavaScript environment takes a little additional setup. The data attribute on the body tag is how we can expose that data to JavaScript from the server side. The easiest way to set environment variables in local development is to put them in a `.env` file. See Appendix A, "Ruby and Rails Setup," for more information on using the `.env` file.

Security Note

Putting the API token in the environment and pulling it through the body tag addresses security from the perspective that we do not put credentials into source code or source code control. We still have an access token visible in the page, though. You could view the source and see the access token. If security is a concern and you want to try to lock down the visibility of credentials in JavaScript, then you need to expose that data through another endpoint over SSL or keep the credential on the server and not exposed to JavaScript at all.

Great! The weather app is now set up to generate maps.

Map Controller

We could put our map in the same controller as the weather charts, but I want to have completely separate routes. The cleanest way to do that is to create a new controller (`rails g controller map index --skip-helper`). We will need two actions like we have for all of the other graphs. The first action will serve the view, and we've created the basis for it with the generator. Once the view is loaded, JavaScript will fire and ask for the data from the second controller action. The Map controller looks like this:

```
class MapController < ApplicationController
  layout "map"

  def index; end
  def map_data
    sql = <<-SQL.strip_heredoc
      SELECT *
      FROM weather_stations
      WHERE station_id IN (
        SELECT DISTINCT station
        FROM weather_readings
        WHERE reading_date < '1837-01-01'
          AND reading_type IN ('TMAX', 'TMIN')
      )
    SQL
    @stations = ActiveRecord::Base.connection.execute(sql)
  end
end
```

You can see on the second line where we specify that we want to use a different layout. The `index` action does not need to do anything. We could omit it completely, but I like to leave it in to communicate that it is there.

The map_data action executes an SQL query. I did not put the query in a model or a database view this time. It is not too long, and it is specific to the mapping aspect of the application. It feels OK here to me. The purpose of the query is to give us the list of weather stations that reported a temperature reading in the year 1836. There are five weather stations that meet those criteria.

Before we leave this section add the route for the map_data action:

```
get 'map/map_data', :defaults => { :format => 'json' }
```

Map Index

The map index is very simple. In fact, I copied one of the existing views for a graph and updated the function. I also made sure that we have a target div to put the map in. The map div has an ID, and generally it is map, but it can be whatever you want it to be (so long as it's valid). Here are the contents of map.html.erb:

```
<script>
$(document).on('ready page:load', function(event) {
  // apply non-idempotent transformations to the body
  makeMap();
});
</script>

<!-- A map will magically appear here -->
<div id="map"></div>
```

While we are thinking about the base page, we should also include the CSS to define how big the map div should be. Here is what app/assets/stylesheets/map.scss looks like:

```
body {
  margin: 0;
  padding: 0;
}
#map {
  position: absolute;
  top: 0;
  bottom: 0;
  width: 100%;
  height: 600px;
}
```

Map Data GeoJSON View

You may have noticed that we did not respond with JSON from the map_data action. That is because we need to format the data in a special JSON format called

GeoJSON. According to GeoJSON.org, "GeoJSON is a format for encoding a variety of geographic data structures." That just means that it's JSON that follows a specific convention for geographic software.

To get our GeoJSON, we will use a JSON builder file for the `map_data` view. A builder file is similar to an ERB file. It has access to the instance variables in the session and knows how to iterate on collections. Builder files are a great way to respond with structured data. XML and JSON builders are fairly common in Rails projects for this reason, especially for an API. For more information on the JSON builder see the JBuilder documentation at https://github.com/rails/jbuilder.

Create a file called `app/views/map/map_data.json.jbuilder`. The contents of the file are as follows:

```
json.type "FeatureCollection"
json.features @stations do |station|
  json.type "Feature"
  json.properties do
    json.set! "marker-color", "#9932CC"
    json.set! "marker-symbol", "circle"
    json.set! "marker-size", "small"
    json.title "#{station['station_id']} (#{station['name']})"
  end
  json.geometry do
    json.type "Point"
    json.coordinates [station['longitude'], station['latitude']]
  end
end
```

The second line iterates on the array of `@stations` that the controller fetched from the database. Each weather station will become a feature in the feature layer we are building. Each feature has properties and a geometry.

The properties are where you define how the feature will look and what information to make available. Here we set the marker color to purple and put a white circle in the marker. We include a property named `title` to identify the feature. You can have as many properties as you need and are free to call them whatever you like. They are especially helpful for grouping and filtering features on the map using D3 selections.

The geometry is what makes this GeoJSON. In Chapter 9, "Working with Geospatial Data in Rails," I discussed some of the geometry data types. Here you can see that this is a point. It has a single coordinate (longitude, latitude).

The formatted JSON response looks like this (except that there are five weather stations in the array):

```
{
  "type": "FeatureCollection",
  "features": [
    {
      "type": "Feature",
      "properties": {
        "marker-color": "#9932CC",
        "marker-symbol": "circle",
        "marker-size": "small",
        "title": "GM000004204 (JENA STERNWARTE)"
      },
      "geometry": {
        "type": "Point",
        "coordinates": [
          "11.5842",
          "50.9267"
        ]
      }
    }
  ]
}
```


The GeoJSON payload for this set of five points is not particularly large. The geometry can potentially be very large though. Imagine listing all of the points required to draw a line around your city, or your country. It would take a lot of points to make the line look correct. You could remove some of the points, which would smooth the line some and reduce the data size.

Smoothing also reduces the fidelity (accuracy) of the geometry. When you are zoomed out you may not notice, but zoom in on a smoothed data set and you will definitely notice. Smoothing is not a technique that I will cover in this book. File this away, and keep it in mind when you see a map slowly paint on your screen. It's probably working pretty hard.

Mapping the Weather Stations

Now the only thing left to do is write the JavaScript to draw the map. We are using the Mapbox Leaflet plug-in. This gives us access to the Mapbox base layer for map imagery. The Mapbox plug-in also adds some additional conveniences and functionality. You will need to create an account and get an access token. Mapbox offers a free starter plan, so you can explore and experiment at no cost. Go ahead and sign up if you haven't already, and make sure to put your API token in a `.env` file or otherwise make it available as an environment variable as discussed above.

The code for our `makeMap()` function looks like this:

```
function makeMap() {
  // initialize the map on the "map" div with a given center and zoom
  L.mapbox.accessToken = $('body').data('mapboxToken');
  var map = L.mapbox.map('map', 'mapbox.streets')
    .setView([39.045753, -76.641273], 9);

  // Create a feature layer with the map_data GeoJSON
  var featureLayer = L.mapbox.featureLayer()
    .loadURL('/map/map_data.json')
    .addTo(map);

  // featureLayer.getBounds() returns the corners of the furthest-out
  // markers. map.fitBounds() makes sure the map contains these.
  featureLayer.on('ready', function(e) {
    map.fitBounds(featureLayer.getBounds());
  });
}
```

There are three phases to this function. The first thing we do is put a map on the page using the `mapbox.streets` base layer. You can see where we tap into the environment variable we stuffed into the body tag to get the access token. With that in place we can now ask Mapbox for a map and its tiles. We also center our map on a coordinate and set the zoom level to `9`.

There are typically 18 zoom levels, but different providers and layers offer different levels of fidelity and zoom. The satellite view is probably going to be the layer with the most constraints based on available photographs. If you pan around a map in the satellite view, you will start seeing different color photographs appear as you cycle through that provider's catalog of available imagery—they were not all taken at the same time.

At this point, if we did nothing else we would have a map that is centered near Baltimore. It would be a very nice map, but it would not display any of our data. That is the second phase of the `makeMap()` function.

A feature layer is just a fancy way of saying another layer on top of the base layer that has features (stuff). The layer is transparent so that it does not interfere with the map tiles on the base layer. The GeoJSON that we fetch from the `map_data` action tells Leaflet where to put our features. The last thing we do in this second phase is add the new feature layer to the map. That does not happen automatically. It is possible to have several layers defined in a map that are not all visible at the same time. This gives our users the capability to choose what they see. In our case, we just have the single layer, and we want it to be visible.

Figure 10.2 Weather Stations Reporting Temperature in 1836

The final phase re-centers the map on our visible markers once the layer is done rendering. The `fitBounds` function also resets the zoom level to show all of our markers. Behind the scenes, Mapbox is drawing something called a **bounding box** around all of the markers. This is simply a rectangle with each corner defined as a coordinate. Those coordinates are used to set the frame and zoom level of the map. We will discuss bounding boxes in more detail in the next chapter.

The map looks like Figure 10.2. Go to http://localhost:3000/map/index to see your map. We loaded the weather readings from 1940 in Chapter 4, "Working with Large Datasets." Try updating the query in the controller to see those weather stations. Hint: look at the `BETWEEN` comparison operator (https://www.postgresql.org/docs/current/static/functions-comparison.html).

Code Checkpoint

To see the code at this stage, go to https://github.com/DataVizToolkit/weather/tree/ch10.1.

Visualizing Airports

The next app that we will work with is the flight departures app. We worked with the departure data in Chapter 6, "The Chord Diagram." Now we are going to turn our attention to the airports.

Markers

The setup for this app is very similar to the previous app. We can start by copying the map layout from the weather app into the layouts folder (`app/views/layouts/map.html.erb`) in this app. Update the title tag in the layout to Airports.

Next we need a new controller, views, and routes. Call the controller `AirportsController`. Go back through the steps from the "Map Controller" section to create the files and routes that you need. You will need to update the `loadURL()` call in `app/assets/javascripts/airports.js` to use the `airports/map_data.json` route. And don't forget to copy over the CSS styles.

There are only two files that we need to change now: the controller and the GeoJSON.

The `map_data` action in the controller needs to get airports from the database. That is a lot of airports. You could pull all of the airports and map them. Leaflet can handle it. It just takes a while to run the query. We do not want to put all of the airports on the map, though. The GeoJSON payload gets pretty large with all those features, too, and chances are nobody would need to see all of the airports at once.

We will instead just get the California airports:

```
@airports = Airport.where(:state => "CA").where("iata !~ '[0-9]'")
```

The second `where` condition filters airports with numbers in the IATA code. That won't catch all the smaller airports, but it catches a lot of them. The GeoJSON view for the airports looks like this:

```
json.type "FeatureCollection"
json.features @airports do |airport|
  json.type "Feature"
  json.properties do
    json.set! "marker-color", "#9932CC"
    json.set! "marker-symbol", "circle"
    json.set! "marker-size", "small"
    json.title "#{airport.airport.squish} (#{airport.iata})"
  end
  json.geometry do
    json.type "Point"
    json.coordinates [airport.longitude, airport.latitude]
  end
end
```

If you run the departures app and go to http://localhost:3000/airports/index you should see Figure 10.3.

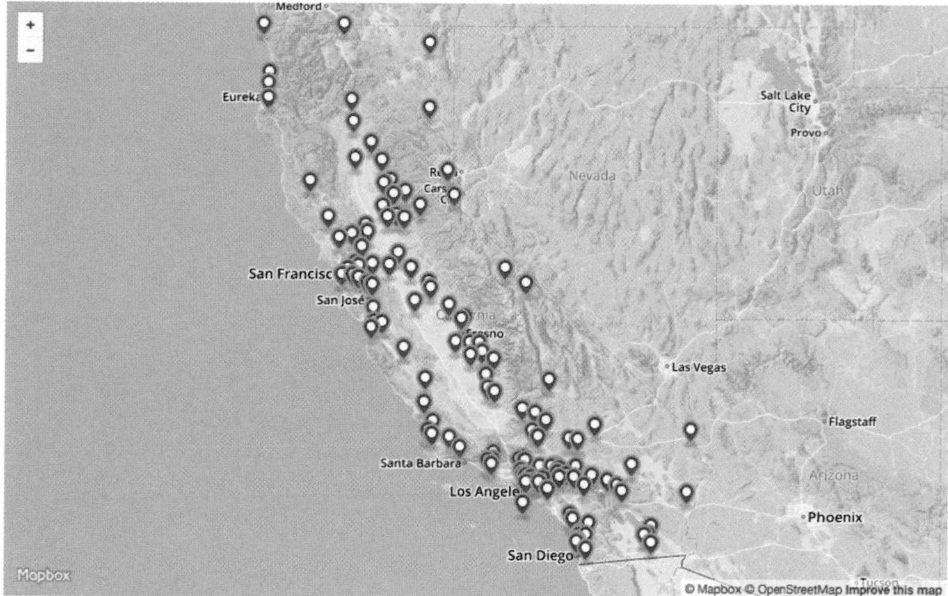

Figure 10.3 California Airport Markers

There are still a lot of markers. We need a strategy for how to handle too much visual information. We need to consolidate the information, which we can do with marker clustering.

Code Checkpoint

To see the code at this stage, go to https://github.com/DataVizToolkit/departures/tree/ch10.1.

Marker Cluster

A marker cluster takes several markers that are close together and consolidates them into a single unit. Generally, you see this as a circle with a number. Leaflet can handle this for us with the Marker Cluster plug-in. We just need to update two files.

First we update the map layout file to include the marker plug-in script and style files. Put these after the Mapbox JavaScript and stylesheet files in the map layout:

```
<%= javascript_include_tag
➥'https://api.mapbox.com/mapbox.js/plugins/leaflet-
➥markercluster/v0.4.0/leaflet.markercluster.js' %>
<%= stylesheet_link_tag
➥'https://api.mapbox.com/mapbox.js/plugins/leaflet-
```

```
➥markercluster/v0.4.0/MarkerCluster.css' %>
<%= stylesheet_link_tag
➥'https://api.mapbox.com/mapbox.js/plugins/leaflet-
➥markercluster/v0.4.0/MarkerCluster.Default.css' %>
```

The second file that we need to update is `airports.js`, where we draw the feature layer. The updated JavaScript looks like this:

```
function makeMap() {
  // initialize the map on the "map" div with a given center and zoom
  L.mapbox.accessToken = $('body').data('mapboxToken');
  var map = L.mapbox.map('map', 'mapbox.streets')
    .setView([39.045753, -76.641273], 9);

  L.mapbox.featureLayer('/airports/map_data.json').on('ready',
➥function(e) {
    var clusterGroup = new L.MarkerClusterGroup({
      maxClusterRadius: 35
    });
    e.target.eachLayer(function(layer) {
      clusterGroup.addLayer(layer);
    });
    map.addLayer(clusterGroup);

    map.fitBounds(clusterGroup.getBounds());
  });
}
```

I rearranged the script a little and took advantage of the fact that Mapbox gives us the capability to pass in a file or a route to `L.mapbox.featureLayer` for the GeoJSON. Rather than define a feature layer for all the markers, we define a marker cluster group. Each cluster is added to the map as a layer. We then get the bounding box for all the clusters together in the cluster group to re-center the map.

Refresh your browser and you should see Figure 10.4.

That's much better. Now we can see where the airports are and how concentrated they are. When you mouseover one of the clusters you can see the boundary represented by that cluster highlighted, like in the Los Angeles area in Figure 10.4.

Code Checkpoint

To see the code at this stage, go to https://github.com/DataVizToolkit/departures/tree/ch10.2.

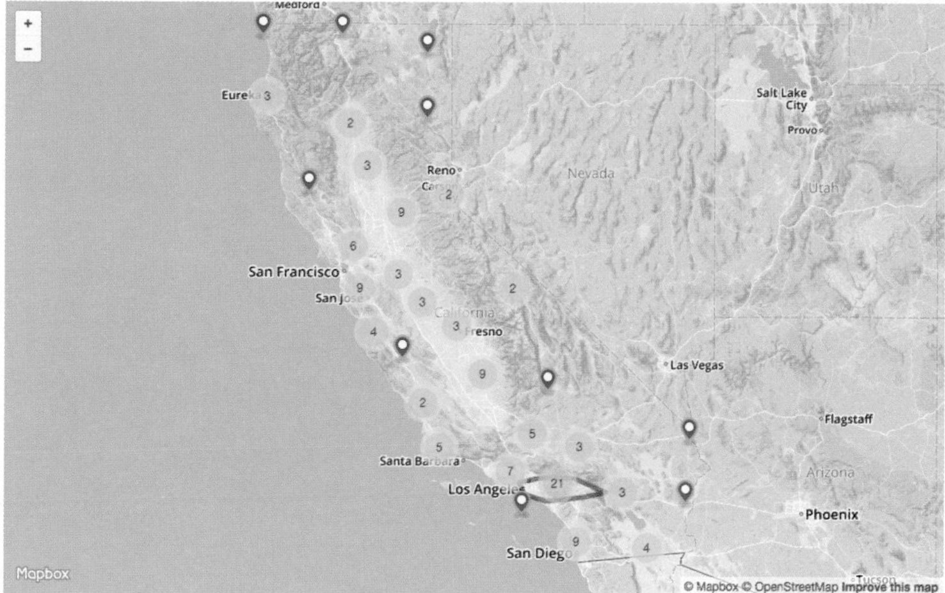

Figure 10.4 California Airport Markers with Marker Clusters

Drawing Flight Paths

The final thing we will do with the airports map is draw an arc between two airports to represent a flight path. It is probably not the actual flight path, but the most direct path, accounting for the curvature of the Earth. The first thing we need to do is include another file from the Mapbox Leaflet plug-in for generating arcs. Add this to the map layout:

```
<%= javascript_include_tag
➥"https://api.mapbox.com/mapbox.js/plugins/arc.js/v0.1.0/arc.js" %>
```

And add this to `airports.js` right before the `map.fitBounds` call:

```
// Add arc between BLH and CEC
var blh = { x: -114.7168764, y: 33.61916278 }
,   cec = { x: -124.2365333, y: 41.78015722 }
,   generator = new arc.GreatCircle(blh, cec, { name: 'BLH to CEC'  })
,   line = generator.Arc(100, { offset: 10  });
L.geoJson(line.json()).addTo(map);
```

When you refresh the map you should see a slightly curved line that goes from an airport at the Northern end of California (CEC—Jack McNamara airport) to the Southern end (BLH—Blythe airport) as in Figure 10.5.

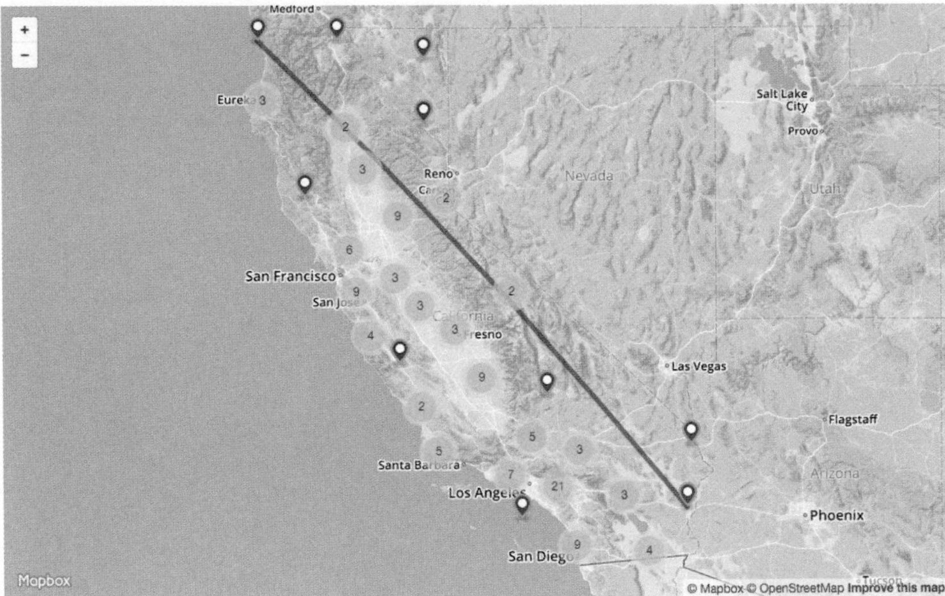

Figure 10.5 Flight Path

Code Checkpoint

To see the code at this stage, go to https://github.com/DataVizToolkit/departures/tree/ch10.3.

Visualizing Zip Codes

The final app we will work with is the Maryland residential sales app. The last thing that we did with this data was in Chapter 5, "Window Functions, Subqueries, and Common Table Expression," where we created a scatter plot of each zip code and its median sales value. We can also visualize the sales data by zip code on a map, and we can use color to signify median value by zip code.

Updating the Maryland Residential Sales App for PostGIS

Before we can map the Maryland zip codes, we need to update the app and database to use PostGIS. There are three things that we need to update to accomplish this:

- Include the `activerecord-postgis-adapter` gem and run `bundle install`
- Update database adapter in `database.yml` to `postgis`
- Run `bundle exec rake db:gis:setup`

Refer to Chapter 9 to see more information on these steps.

Zip Code Geographies

We already have a list of zip codes loaded in the database, but we do not have anything that defines the geographic data of the zip codes. The best thing I found for this is a shapefile. We first discussed shapefiles in Chapter 9.

Zip Code Shapefile

Maryland provides a wealth of GIS data at http://www.mdp.state.md.us/msdc/S5_Map_GIS.shtml. The file we are interested in is the Tiger Shape File for the Zip Code Tabulation Area, which can be found at http://www.mdp.state.md.us/msdc/census/cen2010/maps/tiger10/zcta2010.zip. After you download the zip file, you need to unzip the contents into a directory. You can do that from the command line with the `unzip` command:

```
unzip zcta2010.zip -d tmp/maryland
```

The projected coordinate system for the shapefile is something we have not encountered yet: NAD83 State Plane Maryland FIPS 1900 (meters). This is not a projection that we can work with directly. We need to re-project this shapefile from the NAD83 datum to the WGS84 datum before we can import the data. The `4326` SRID is a WGS84 projection, and that's the one that we want to use for this data.

Re-projecting the Zip Code Shapefile

Changing the projection of a shapefile requires some extra software. My initial searches for the Maryland data kept turning up ExpertGPS. I've never used ExpertGPS, though, so I cannot speak to its functionality or ease of use. However, I have used QGIS (formerly Quantum GIS), and that's what I will use for this task. QGIS is available for Windows, OS X, Linux, and Android. Go to QGIS.org to find the installation method for your platform. I am using version 2.14.0 in these examples.

Once you have QGIS installed and running, open the shapefile you downloaded. Navigate to the `tmp/maryland/zctz_statewide_shoreline.shp` file in the Browser Panel and open it. When you do you should see an option window that looks like Figure 10.6. Find the entry for EPSG:102285 (NAD83 State Plane Maryland FIPS 1900) and select OK.

You should see the outline of Maryland and all of the counties on a white backdrop. This shapefile is just Maryland, so you will not see the rest of the United States or the Atlantic Ocean. To export the layer in a different projection we need to save it as a new layer. In the top menu choose Layer and then Save As.

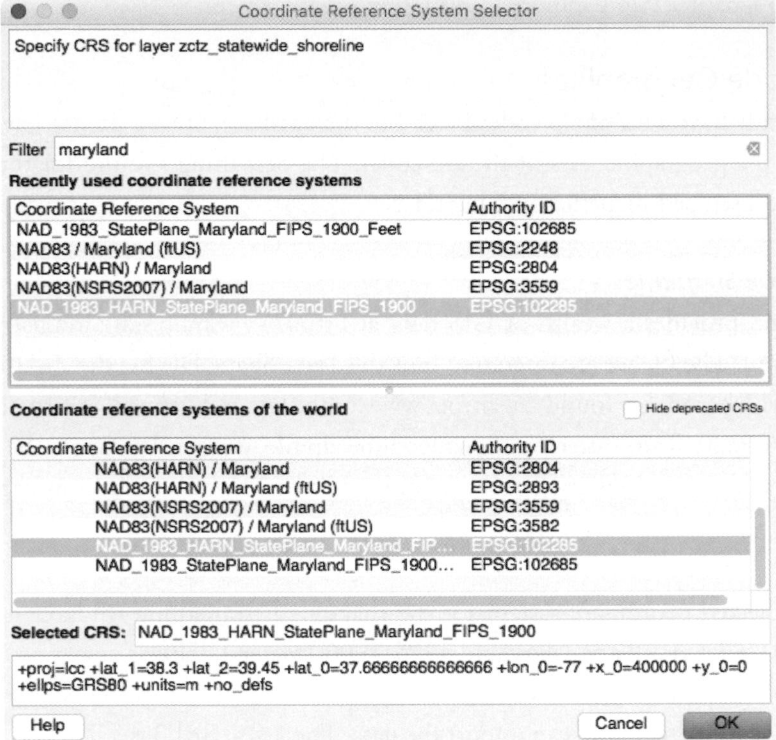

Figure 10.6 QGIS Import Dialog

Choose a location to save the file. I exported mine back into the `tmp/maryland` directory. You also need to choose a projection. Select "Default CRS (EPSG: 4326 - WGS 84)." I outlined the two options you need to set in the export dialog in Figure 10.7.

Once you've made those selections click OK, and you've got a re-projected shapefile!

Importing the Zip Code Shapefile

Now that we have a shapefile in the projection we want we use the `shp2pgsql` command that we used in Chapter 9 to import the data:

```
shp2pgsql -s 4326 -d \
  tmp/maryland/zipcodes.shp \
  zipcodes | psql -h localhost \
  -d residential_sales_development -U barrettclark
```

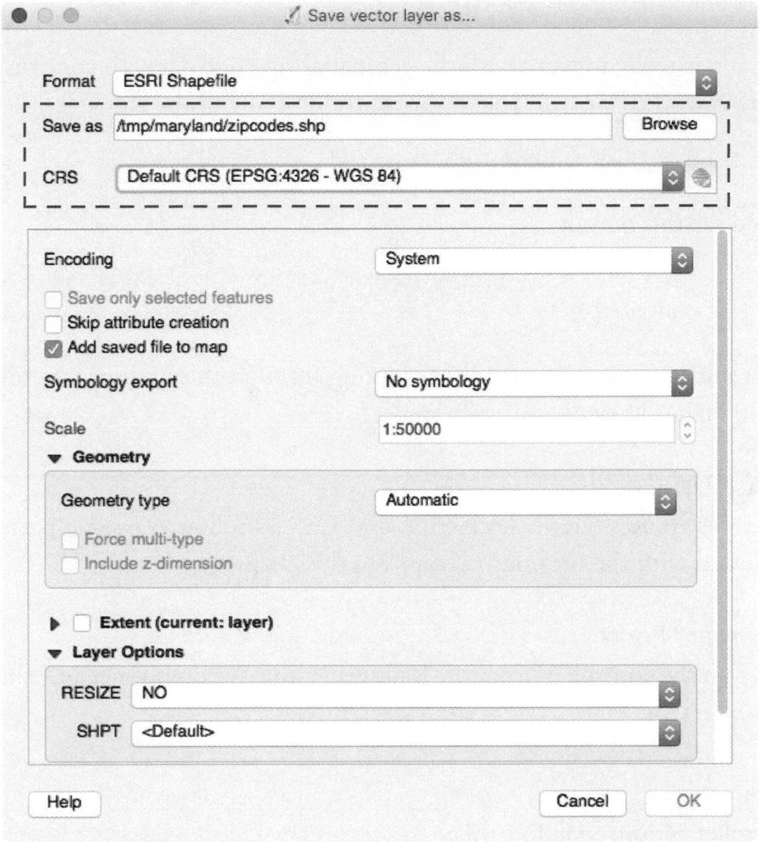

Figure 10.7 QGIS Export Dialog

Be sure you use your database username instead of mine, and change the file path if you put the `.shp` file elsewhere. You should see `INSERT 0 1` printed to your terminal several times if the import works.

When the import finishes you will have a new zip codes table that you do not have a migration for. The database structure file is out of sync with the database, so let's get it caught up by running:

```
bundle exec rake db:structure:dump
```

We also want a model file so we can make full use of the data in ActiveRecord and Rails. We use the Rails model generator to accomplish this, and we tell it to skip the migration because the table already exists.

```
rails g model zipcode --skip-migration
```

Now our app is ready to work with the geospatial zip code data. To confirm that the re-projection worked we can look at the centroid of one of the zip codes:

```
Zipcode.find_by(:zcta5ce10 => "21529").geom.centroid
```

You should see this output:

```
#<RGeo::Geos::CAPIPointImpl:0x3fbfcf965e64 "POINT (-78.76859885632825
➥39.706068328507996)">
```

I got it wrong a couple of times while working through this and saw coordinates in the 20,000 range! They did not map well.

Mapping Zip Codes

The controller, routes, views, JavaScript, and CSS all follow the same patterns that we've followed with the previous two apps in this chapter.

Controller and Routes

We can set up the controller using the Rails generator. We do not need the helper file so we can skip that.

```
rails g controller map --skip-helper
```

The controller actions look like this:

```
  def index; end
  def map_data
    @zipcodes = SalesFigure.zipcode_data
  end
```

The routes look like this:

```
  get 'map/index'
  get 'map/map_data', :defaults => { :format => 'json' }
```

View Files

We will use the application layout in this app. Add these two lines after D3 is included:

```
<%= javascript_include_tag
➥"https://api.tiles.mapbox.com/mapbox.js/v2.2.4/mapbox.js" %>
<%= stylesheet_link_tag
➥"https://api.tiles.mapbox.com/mapbox.js/v2.2.4/mapbox.css" %>
```

jQuery, D3, and Leaflet can all happily co-exist. Be sure that you also add the Mapbox token in the body tag of the layout:

```
<body data-mapbox-token="<%= ENV['MAPBOX_TOKEN'] %>">
```

The map view file (`app/views/map/index.html.erb`) looks like this:

```
<script>
$(document).on('ready page:load', function(event) {
  // apply non-idempotent transformations to the body
  makeMap();
});
</script>

<!-- A map will magically appear here -->
<div id="map"></div>
```

The stylesheet looks like this:

```
body {
  margin: 0;
  padding: 0;
}
#map {
  position: absolute;
  top: 0;
  bottom: 0;
  width: 100%;
  height: 600px;
}
.map-legend ul {
  list-style: none;
  padding-left: 0;
}
.map-legend .swatch {
  width: 20px;
  height: 20px;
  float: left;
  margin-right: 10px;
}
.leaflet-popup-close-button {
  display: none;
}
.leaflet-popup-content-wrapper {
  pointer-events: none;
}
```

Finally, add the JavaScript in `app/assets/javascripts/map.js`:

```
function makeMap() {
  // initialize the map on the "map" div with a given center and zoom
  L.mapbox.accessToken = $('body').data('mapboxToken');
  var map = L.mapbox.map('map', 'mapbox.streets')
    .setView([39.045753, -76.641273], 9);

  var featureLayer = L.mapbox.featureLayer()
    .loadURL('/map/map_data.json')
    .addTo(map);

  // featureLayer.getBounds() returns the corners of the furthest-out
  // markers. map.fitBounds() makes sure the map contains these.
  featureLayer.on('ready', function(e) {
    map.fitBounds(featureLayer.getBounds());
  });
}
```

The Data

Now we need to write the query to retrieve and format the data. You can put the query in the model or in the controller. In this app I went with a class method in the `SalesFigure` model:

```
def self.zipcode_data
  sql = <<-SQL
    SELECT sales.id, sales.zipcode, sales.jurisdiction,
      sales.total_sales, sales.median_value, z.gid, z.statefp10,
      z.zcta5ce10, z.geoid10, z.classfp10, z.mtfcc10, z.funcstat10,
      ST_AsGeoJSON(z.geom)::JSON AS geometry
    FROM sales_figures sales
    JOIN zipcodes z ON sales.zipcode = z.zcta5ce10
  SQL
  connection.execute(sql)
end
```

I have introduced another PostGIS function in this query with `ST_AsGeoJSON`. If you look at one of the zip code records and all of its coordinates, you'll see the geometry (`geom`) column parsed into coordinates. These are actually stored in a different format in the database. We need to translate that `geometry` datatype to a **well-known text** (WKT) representation. We also need our data in GeoJSON format, and PostGIS can do that for us.

You could also add the model associations if you like. We will not be using those associations in this app, but it never hurts to be clear and document where there are relationships. In the `SalesFigure` model:

```
has_many :zipcodes, :primary_key => :zipcode, :foreign_key => :zcta5ce10
```

And then in `Zipcode` the inverse would be:

```
belongs_to :sales_figure, :primary_key => :zipcode, :foreign_key => :zc-
        ta5ce10
```

The only other thing to do now is format the data. We will use JBuilder again. This is what `app/views/map/map_data.json.jbuilder` looks like:

```
json.type "FeatureCollection"
json.features @zipcodes do |zipcode|
  json.type "Feature"
  json.id Integer(zipcode["id"])
  json.properties do
    json.zipcode zipcode["zipcode"]
    json.county zipcode["jurisdiction"]
    json.total_sales Integer(zipcode["total_sales"])
    json.median_value Integer(zipcode["median_value"])
  end
  json.geometry JSON.parse(zipcode["geometry"])
end
```

In this response we send a little more data back in the `properties` section of the GeoJSON. That gives the front-end more information that it can display and also more information to determine how each zip code is rendered. We could define the display coloring in the JSON, but we will do that in the JavaScript soon. The other thing we do is parse the GeoJSON geometry that we pulled from the database. Even though we wrote the query to return JSON, it comes out of the database as a string, and we need to coerce it back into JSON. Type coercion is one of the magical things that ActiveRecord handles for you behind the scenes when you use a model to execute queries. Since we are not using that functionality we need to perform the coercion ourselves. You can see where we also coerced the `id` to an `Integer`.

Great! Now you should have all the pieces in place to see the Maryland zip codes. Once they finish loading, they should be grey and look like Figure 10.8.

Code Checkpoint

To see the code at this stage, go to https://github.com/DataVizToolkit/residential_sales/tree/ch10.1.

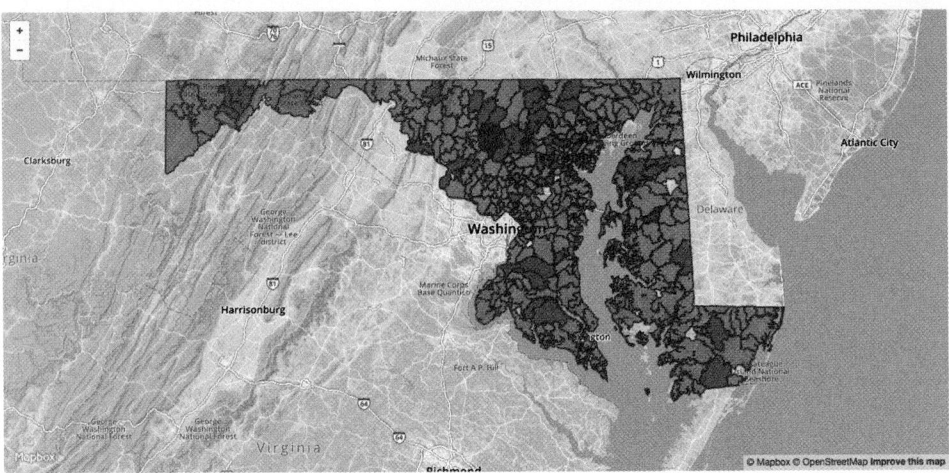

Figure 10.8 Maryland Zip Codes

Choropleth

A choropleth map is a thematic map in which areas are shaded or patterned in proportion to the measurement of the statistical variable being displayed on the map, such as population density or per-capita income. They can convey a lot of information in a simple map and also be visually appealing.

Converting our grey zip codes into a colorful choropleth requires updating the `makeMap()` function. We will do this in two passes. First let's add a splash of color. Here is what `makeMap()` looks like:

```
function makeMap() {
  // initialize the map on the "map" div with a given center and zoom
  L.mapbox.accessToken = $('body').data('mapboxToken');
  var map = L.mapbox.map('map', 'mapbox.streets')
    .setView([39.045753, -76.641273], 9);

  var featureLayer = L.mapbox.featureLayer()
    .loadURL('/map/map_data.json')
    .addTo(map);

  var getStyle = function(feature) {
    return {
      weight: 2,
      opacity: 0.1,
      color: 'black',
      fillOpacity: 0.7,
      fillColor: getColor(feature.properties.median_value)
    };
```

```
  }
  var getColor = function(value) {
    return value > 750000 ? "#8c2d04" :
           value > 500000 ? "#cc4c02" :
           value > 400000 ? "#ec7014" :
           value > 300000 ? "#fe9929" :
           value > 200000 ? "#fec44f" :
           value > 100000 ? "#fee391" :
           value >  50000 ? "#fff7bc" :
                            "#ffffe5"
  };

  // featureLayer.getBounds() returns the corners of the furthest-out
  // markers. map.fitBounds() makes sure the map contains these.
  featureLayer.on('ready', function(e) {
    featureLayer.eachLayer(function(layer) {
      var medianValue = layer.feature.properties.median_value;
      layer.setStyle(getStyle(layer.feature));
    });
    map.fitBounds(featureLayer.getBounds());
  });
}
```

A lot of this should look familiar by now. The `getStyle` and `getColor` functions are new. We grab the median value from the GeoJSON properties and use that to set the color. The darker the color, the higher the median value. The choropleth is taking shape! You should see a map that looks like Figure 10.9.

The colors are pretty, and I confess that I could look at these all day long. We can make it even more interesting, though. Let's add in some interactivity with popups that appear when you mouseover each zip code. We will also add the ability to click on a zip code to zoom in and see the zip code in closer detail. We should add a legend, too.

I have adapted the Mapbox choropleth example (https://www.mapbox.com/mapbox.js/example/v1.0.0/choropleth).

```
function makeMap() {
  // initialize the map on the "map" div with a given center and zoom
  L.mapbox.accessToken = $('body').data('mapboxToken');
  var map = L.mapbox.map('map', 'mapbox.streets')
    .setView([39.045753, -76.641273], 9);

  var featureLayer = L.mapbox.featureLayer()
    .loadURL('/map/map_data.json')
    .addTo(map);

  var popup = new L.Popup({ autoPan: false  });
```

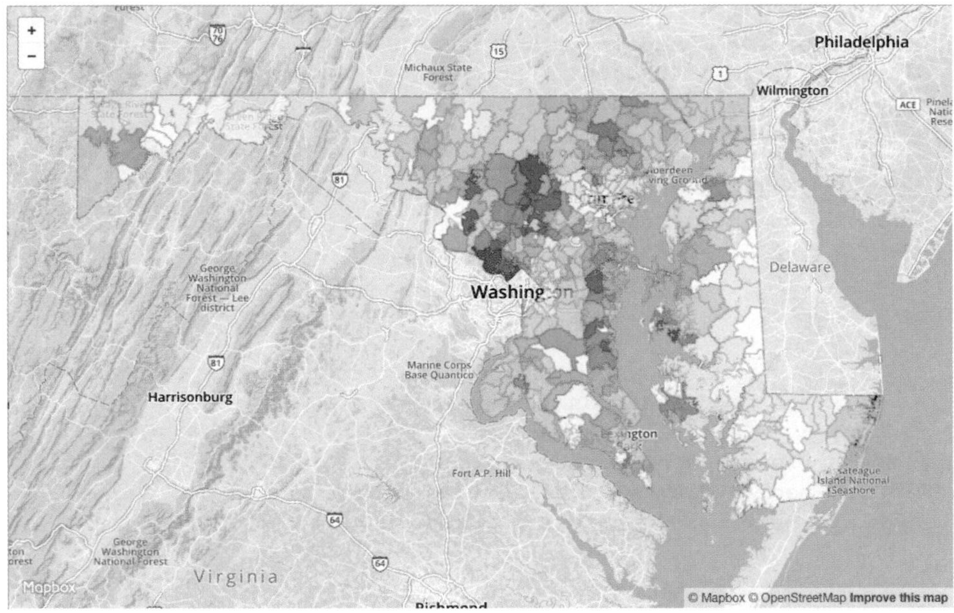

Figure 10.9 Maryland Zip Code Choropleth

```
var closeTooltip;
var zoomToFeature = function(e) {
  map.fitBounds(e.target.getBounds());
}
var mousemove = function(e) {
  var layer = e.target;

  popup.setLatLng(e.latlng);
  popup.setContent('<div class="marker-title">Zipcode: ' +
➥layer.feature.properties.zipcode + '</div>' +
      'Median value: $' + layer.feature.properties.median_value);

  if (!popup._map) popup.openOn(map);
  window.clearTimeout(closeTooltip);

  // highlight feature
  layer.setStyle({
    weight: 3,
    opacity: 0.3,
    fillOpacity: 0.9
  });

  if (!L.Browser.ie && !L.Browser.opera) {
    layer.bringToFront();
  }
}
```

```
var mouseout = function(e) {
  var layer = e.target;
  layer.setStyle(getStyle(layer.feature));
  closeTooltip = window.setTimeout(function() {
    map.closePopup();
  }, 100);
}

var getStyle = function(feature) {
  return {
    weight: 2,
    opacity: 0.1,
    color: 'black',
    fillOpacity: 0.7,
    fillColor: getColor(feature.properties.median_value)
  };
}
var getColor = function(value) {
  return value > 750000 ? "#8c2d04" :
         value > 500000 ? "#cc4c02" :
         value > 400000 ? "#ec7014" :
         value > 300000 ? "#fe9929" :
         value > 200000 ? "#fec44f" :
         value > 100000 ? "#fee391" :
         value >  50000 ? "#fff7bc" :
                          "#ffffe5"
};

function getLegendHTML() {
  var grades = [0, 50000, 100000, 200000, 300000, 400000, 500000,
➥750000],
  labels = [],
  from, to;

  for (var i = 0; i < grades.length; i++) {
    from = grades[i];
    to = grades[i + 1];

    labels.push(
      '<li><span class="swatch" style="background:' + getColor(from +
➥1) + '"></span> ' +
      '$' + from + (to ? '&ndash;$' + to : '+')) + '</li>';
  }

  return '<span>Median Value</span><ul>' + labels.join('') + '</ul>';
}

// featureLayer.getBounds() returns the corners of the furthest-out
// markers. map.fitBounds() makes sure the map contains these.
```

```
  featureLayer.on('ready', function(e) {
    featureLayer.eachLayer(function(layer) {
      var medianValue = layer.feature.properties.median_value;
      layer.on({
        mousemove: mousemove,
        mouseout: mouseout,
        click: zoomToFeature
      });
      layer.setStyle(getStyle(layer.feature));
    });
    map.legendControl.addLegend(getLegendHTML());
    map.fitBounds(featureLayer.getBounds());
  });
}
```

We also need to add a little more CSS to make the legend and popups look correct. Add this to `map.scss`:

```
.map-legend ul {
  list-style: none;
  padding-left: 0;
}
.map-legend .swatch {
  width: 20px;
  height: 20px;
  float: left;
  margin-right: 10px;
}
.leaflet-popup-close-button {
  display: none;
```

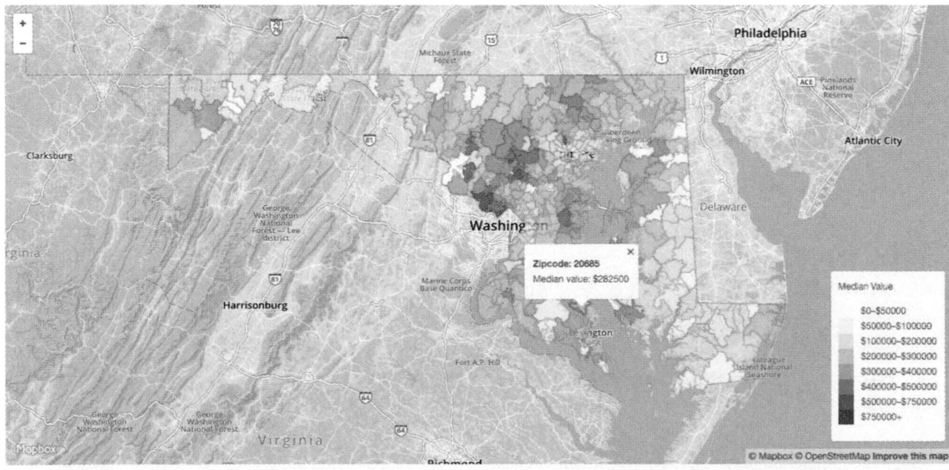

Figure 10.10 Full Maryland Zip Code Choropleth

```
}
.leaflet-popup-content-wrapper {
  pointer-events: none;
}
```

Now when you refresh the page you should see a beautiful and interactive choropleth (Figure 10.10)!

Code Checkpoint

To see the code at this stage, go to https://github.com/DataVizToolkit/residential_sales/tree/ch10.2.

Summary

In this chapter we reviewed how to configure an app and database for PostGIS and we learned about the Leaflet JavaScript mapping library. We updated all three of the apps that we've been working on throughout the book to draw relevant maps. We put pins on the map to show where the five weather stations that reported temperature in 1836 are located. We highlighted where the California airports are located and learned about marker clusters to handle high concentrations of markers. Finally, we drew the boundaries of the Maryland zip codes and turned that map into a choropleth to show the median value of houses sold in each zip code.

Chapter 11
Querying Geospatial Data

You can store a latitude and longitude in your database and make maps without PostGIS. We cannot, however, ask spatial questions of our data unless the database understands spatial concepts. That's where PostGIS and the spatial SQL functions provided by PostGIS come into play.

In this chapter we look at the two most common spatial questions you will need to ask of your data: "What exists in this area?" and "What exists near this point?" Before we can answer the first question we need to discuss how to define that area. For that we use something called a bounding box.

Finding Items within a Bounding Box

Imagine that you are a logistics coordinator and you are responsible for the whereabouts of all of the assets that your company manages. You would like to know where your stuff is, right? What equipment is safely stored in the storage yard, and what equipment is stationed at the various work sites?

We can answer those questions easily by defining each location and giving it a polygon or multipolygon that represents its boundary. We can then use that geometry as a *bounding box* and find all records that fall inside.

What Is a Bounding Box?

We first touched on the bounding box in the previous chapter, "Making Maps with Leaflet and Rails." As a refresher, a bounding box, also known as a bbox or an envelope, is a rectangle with each corner defined as a coordinate. The bounding box surrounds a geographic feature. The feature is therefore bounded by this imaginary box.

The bounding box is one of the fundamental concepts in GIS. Remember in Chapter 10 where we issued this statement:

```
map.fitBounds(featureLayer.getBounds())
```

It asked the map for the bounding box of all the features in the map, and then set the zoom level of the map to that bounding box.

Writing a Bounding Box Query

As you have seen through previous chapters, we have a couple of ways that we can construct a query that calculates a bounding box for us. We can use PostGIS directly, or we can let the ActiveRecord PostGIS adapter do it for us.

Writing a Bounding Box Query Using SQL and PostGIS

My preferred way to use PostGIS is directly via SQL. That is probably because I learned the PostGIS spatial SQL functions first before the RGeo gem and Active-Record PostGIS adapter were fully baked. The ActiveRecord adapter sits on top of the RGeo gem, and they've both evolved a lot and are quite good now.

However, there is still not a direct mapping of all the PostGIS functions to the ActiveRecord PostGIS adapter. The documentation even tells us that "if you want to perform a spatial query, you'll look for, say, all the points within a given area. For those queries, you'll need to use the standard spatial SQL functions provided by Post-GIS." So you can decide for yourself how much you want to straddle that line. I present both options of using PostGIS directly or within ActiveRecord in this chapter.

Here is a query that displays a zip code and the bounding box formatted as well-known text (WKT). The actual envelope is a geometry, which is not human readable.

```
SELECT zcta5ce10,
  ST_AsText(ST_Envelope(geom)) AS bbox_wkt
FROM zipcodes
LIMIT 1;
```

```
 zcta5ce10 |                                                    bbox_wkt
-----------+--------------------------------------------------------------
➥------------------------------------------------------------------------
➥------------------

 21529     | POLYGON((-78.789527 39.6780049999998,-78.789527
➥39.7230169999998,-78.742523 39.7230169999998,-78.742523
➥39.6780049999998,-78.789527 39.6780049999998))
 (1 row)
```

You may have noticed that I said a bounding box has four corners, each with a coordinate, and there are five points in that envelope. The fifth point is the same as the first point, which closes the bounding box and makes it a `POLYGON`.

Writing a Bounding Box Query Using ActiveRecord

We can also let ActiveRecord and RGeo calculate the envelope for us. To see that we can run this in `rails console`:

```
>> zipcode = Zipcode.first; nil
  Zipcode Load (0.8ms)  SELECT  "zipcodes".* FROM "zipcodes"  ORDER BY
➥"zipcodes"."gid" ASC LIMIT 1
=> nil
>> zipcode.geom.envelope
=> #<RGeo::Geos::CAPIPolygonImpl:0x3fd4ff8c5adc "POLYGON ((-78.789527
➥39.67800499999982, -78.74252300000002 39.67800499999982, -
➥78.74252300000002 39.72301699999982, -78.789527 39.72301699999982, -
➥78.789527 39.67800499999982))">
```

Both methods for calculating an envelope are pretty simple and straightforward. You can choose whichever way works best for you when you need to create a bounding box. It's good to have choices!

Finding Items within the Bounding Box

Now that we have a bounding box we can find zip codes that fall inside it. We need to be specific about what we mean by that though. A point or polygon can be fully contained within the bounding box, or it can simply overlap (intersect) it.

This first query will return any record that is fully contained within the bounding box. You can see that it returns a single zip code, which is good because we are using that zip code's bounding box.

```
-- @ is contained by
SELECT zcta5ce10
FROM zipcodes
WHERE geom @
 ST_Envelope('POLYGON ((
  -78.789527 39.67800499999982,
  -78.74252300000002 39.67800499999982,
  -78.74252300000002 39.72301699999982,
  -78.789527 39.72301699999982,
  -78.789527 39.67800499999982))'::geometry);

 zcta5ce10
-----------
 21529
(1 row)
```

The other way we can run this query is to ask for any record that has a geometry that intersects, or overlaps, the bounding box. It just takes a single point to fall within the bounding box for another geometry to be considered intersecting.

```
-- && is intersects
SELECT zcta5ce10
FROM zipcodes
WHERE geom &&
 ST_Envelope('POLYGON ((
  -78.789527 39.67800499999982,
  -78.74252300000002 39.67800499999982,
  -78.74252300000002 39.72301699999982,
  -78.789527 39.72301699999982,
  -78.789527 39.67800499999982))'::geometry);

 zcta5ce10
-----------
 21529
 21502
 21524
(3 rows)
```

Here you can see that there are two other zip codes that overlap the source zip code's bounding box. Note that we are not comparing each zip code's bounding box to the source bounding box. We are looking at each zip code's geometry.

We can run the same query in Rails. RGeo does not give us a helper method, so we need to put the spatial SQL for the `WHERE` clause into the ActiveRecord finder method.

First we will run the "contained" query using the `&&` operator in `rails console`:

```
>> zipcode = Zipcode.first; nil
  Zipcode Load (0.8ms)  SELECT  "zipcodes".* FROM "zipcodes"  ORDER BY
➥"zipcodes"."gid" ASC LIMIT 1
=> nil
>> zipcodes = Zipcode.where("geom && ?", zipcode.geom.envelope); nil
=> nil
>> zipcodes.map(&:zcta5ce10)
  Zipcode Load (10.8ms)  SELECT "zipcodes".* FROM "zipcodes" WHERE
➥(geom &&
➥'0020000003000010e60000000100000005c053b2879c4113c74043d6c8de2ac309c053af
➥857f3061c94043d6c8de2ac309c053af857f3061c94043dc8bd230b9c3c053b2879c4113c
➥74043dc8bd230b9c3c053b2879c4113c74043d6c8de2ac309')
=> ["21529", "21502", "21524"]
```

The question mark (?) that you see in the query is what ActiveRecord uses to substitute values into a query. You could put the variable directly in the query, but using the question mark placeholder offers added security to avoid SQL injection because ActiveRecord sanitizes the values it substitutes into your queries.

Next we will run the "includes" query using the @ operator in `rails console`:

```
>> zipcodes = Zipcode.where("geom @ ?", zipcode.geom.envelope); nil
=> nil
>> zipcodes.map(&:zcta5ce10)
  Zipcode Load (10.2ms)  SELECT "zipcodes".* FROM "zipcodes" WHERE
➥(geom @
➥'0020000003000010e6000000010000005c053b2879c4113c74043d6c8de2ac309c053af
➥857f3061c94043d6c8de2ac309c053af857f3061c94043dc8bd230b9c3c053b2879c4113c
➥74043dc8bd230b9c3c053b2879c4113c74043d6c8de2ac309')
=> ["21529"]
```

The envelope in the queries was not displayed in WKT format but instead as a geometry. The WKT representation is for us to be able to see the attributes of the geometry.

Finding Items Near a Point

We are going to switch gears from zip codes to airports and the departures app now. Imagine that you need to build a flight search page. The typical inputs for that are departure date, return date, origin airport, and destination airport. That's called "the cannonball" in travel jargon.

You type in "San Francisco" and "New York City" for the origin and destination. Those aren't airports, though. We need to know that San Francisco means SFO. Furthermore, New York City could mean several things. There are three airports in the NYC area, and there is also a code for the NYC area in general.

Our app doesn't know any of that. We need to teach it.

Writing the Query

Step 1 (for our airports table) is to make sure we have filled in the `lonlat` values. We added a migration in Chapter 9, "Working with Geospatial Data in Rails." If you have not run that migration yet be sure that you do so before proceeding. Alternately you can run this query in your favorite SQL editor, which you may need to do if you ran all the migrations before loading the data:

```
UPDATE airports
SET lonlat = ST_GeomFromText('POINT(' || long || ' ' || lat || ')',4326)
WHERE lonlat IS NULL;
```

With all the data in place we can ask a question of the database: *List the three airports that are closest to San Francisco.*

We cap the search radius at 200 miles so that in less dense areas we do not recommend an airport that is too far away. Note that this distance is as the crow flies, not driving distance.

```
SELECT ST_Distance(
  lonlat,
  ST_GeomFromText('POINT(-122.3748433 37.61900194)',4326)
) AS distance_meters, id, iata, airport, city, state, country
FROM airports
WHERE ST_DWithin(
  -- geom 1
  lonlat,
  -- geom 2
  ST_GeomFromText('POINT(-122.3748433 37.61900194)',4326),
  -- distance in meters (200 miles)
  200 * 1609.34
)
ORDER BY 1
LIMIT 3;
```

```
 distance_meters |  id  | iata |           airport            |     city
➥| state | country
-----------------+------+------+------------------------------+-----------
➥----+-------+---------
      5.22691384 | 2935 | SFO  | San Francisco International | San
➥Francisco | CA    | USA
  16144.85676752 | 1689 | HAF  | Half Moon Bay                | Half Moon
➥Bay | CA     | USA
  16248.23050337 | 3007 | SQL  | San Carlos                   | San Carlos
➥| CA     | USA
(3 rows)
```

The query calculates the distance from each record's `lonlat` to a point in San Francisco using the `ST_Distance` function. We also sort by that calculated field, which is the first field in the query. We limit the search radius to 200 miles by using the `ST_DWithin` function in the `WHERE` clause. Again, for that function we compare each record's `lonlat` value to that point in San Francisco. Distances are in meters with both of these functions, and a mile is 1609.34 meters. You could, of course, just put 321868 instead of doing the calculation.

Using ActiveRecord

Finding items near a point is another one of those areas where we need to fall back to using the standard spatial SQL functions. We can make it more "railsy" by including the SQL from the `WHERE` clause as a scope in the `Airport` model.

```
scope :close_to, -> (lon, lat, distance_in_meters = 200 * 1609.34) {
  select(sanitize_sql_array([%{
    ST_Distance(
      lonlat,
      ST_GeomFromText('POINT(? ?)',4326)
    ) AS distance_meters,
    *
  }, lon, lat])).
  where( [%{
    ST_DWithin(
      lonlat,
      ST_GeographyFromText('SRID=4326;POINT(? ?)'),
      ?
    )
  }, lon, lat, distance_in_meters]).
  order("1")
}
```

The syntax in that scope may look a little strange. We use `%{}` to quote the text of the query. You could also use a heredoc instead of the quoting literal. The quote literal is more compact and fits better in the scope. We also use field order for sorting in this query. Passing the string `"1"` to ActiveRecord's `order` enables us to use field order sorting like we did in the raw SQL example.

With the scope in the model we can then run the query like this in `rails console`:

```
>> sfo = Airport.find_by(:iata => "SFO"); nil
  Airport Load (3.6ms)  SELECT  "airports".* FROM "airports" WHERE
➥airports"."iata" = $1  ORDER BY "airports"."id" ASC LIMIT 1
➥[["iata", "SFO"]]
=> nil
>> airports = Airport.close_to(sfo.long, sfo.lat).limit(3)
  Airport Load (9.7ms)  SELECT
      ST_Distance(
        lonlat,
        ST_GeomFromText('POINT(-122.374889 37.618972)',4326)
      ) AS distance_meters,
      *
     FROM "airports" WHERE (
      ST_DWithin(
```

```
        lonlat,
        ST_GeographyFromText('SRID=4326;POINT(-122.374889 37.618972)'),
        321868.0
      )
  )  ORDER BY 1 LIMIT 3
```

This does everything that we need it to do. We can look at the three airports we got back from the query to see how far each airport is from SFO:

```
>> airports.map(&:distance_meters)
=> [5.22691384, 16139.66651997, 16248.55195813]
```

The first airport in the array is SFO. The two other airports are HAF and SQL, same as before when we ran the query using raw SQL.

If the scope option works well for you, then go for it. For a general query that needs to get the nearest places I think the spatial SQL query is clearer and easier to implement.

Code Checkpoint

To see the code at this stage, go to https://github.com/DataVizToolkit/departures/tree/ch11.1.

Calculating Distance

I first touched on distance calculations in Chapter 9, "Working with Geospatial Data in Rails." I used `ST_Distance` in the query to find the nearest airports earlier in this chapter. It's the PostGIS function that I use the most.

Bear in mind that each projection carries with it some level of distortion. You're taking the globe, or some section of it, and projecting it onto a flat surface. Distance can, therefore, be distorted because the projection is distorted. It may be less pronounced if you're using a localized projection.

The precise distance may or may not be a concern. The `ST_Distance` value might be good enough. You can always run a comparison with a sampling of your data to compare `ST_Distance` against `ST_Distance_Spherical`.

For a comparison of the distance methods, adapted from the example in the PostGIS documentation (http://postgis.net/docs/ST_Distance_Spheroid.html), you can run the following query that calculates the distance to San Francisco from each airport:

```
SELECT
  iata AS origin,
  'SFO' AS destination,
```

```
  ST_DistanceSpheroid(
    lonlat::geometry,
    ST_GeomFromText('POINT(-122.3748433 37.61900194)',4326),
    'SPHEROID["WGS 84",6378137,298.257223563]'
  )::numeric AS dist_meters_spheroid,
  ST_DistanceSphere(
    lonlat::geometry,
    ST_GeomFromText('POINT(-122.3748433 37.61900194)',4326)
  )::numeric AS dist_meters_sphere,
  ST_Distance(
    lonlat,
    ST_GeomFromText('POINT(-122.3748433 37.61900194)',4326)
  )::numeric AS dist_meters
FROM airports
ORDER BY 3, 4, 5;

origin | destination | dist_meters_spheroid | dist_meters_sphere  |
➥dist_meters
--------+-------------+----------------------+--------------------+-
➥---------------
 SFO    | SFO         |                    0 |                  0 |
➥0
 HAF    | SFO         |     16144.8567675205 |     16142.42401246 |
➥16144.85676752
 SQL    | SFO         |     16248.2305033691 |     16246.67141856 |
➥16248.23050337
 OAK    | SFO         |     17714.1248877347 |     17702.88462401 |
➥17714.12488773
 HWD    | SFO         |     22723.9299351756 |     22673.89418423 |
➥22723.92993518
...
X67     | SFO         |     5997749.13498262 |   5990953.06645244 |
➥5997749.13498262
 SPN    | SFO         |     9181695.29244502 |   9169310.18933521 |
➥9181695.29244502
 YAP    | SFO         |     10199502.8283456 |   10188195.2826943 |
➥10199502.8283456
 ROR    | SFO         |     10653566.2887779 |   10642652.2232187 |
➥10653566.2887779
 ROP    | SFO         |     12691125.3698576 |   12674444.9697885 |
➥12691125.3698576
```

Summary

This chapter was heavy on queries and ActiveRecord. I went over the two questions that I need to answer the most when working with geospatial data: "What exists in this area?" and "What exists near this point?" Before we could get too far into the first question we first needed to cover the bounding box.

There is more that we can do with these concepts. You can add functionality to a map to capture the coordinate location for a click (or touch) in the map. Given that coordinate you can search for nearby points of interest. You can also add drawing tools to a map to draw a bounding box or even create new geometries.

The sky is the limit, and you now have the necessary foundation to go and create your own fantastic geospatial applications.

Afterword

This book contains most of what I know how to do with data. I told you in the Preface that I love data. I like playing with it—cleaning the data up and then letting it tell a story. I hope that enthusiasm came through in my writing, and I hope that the information is useful to you.

This may be the end of the book, but it is not the end of the story. Take what you've learned and go make your own data dance.

Appendix A
Ruby and Rails Setup

This appendix is a brief overview of all the little things that go into getting your environment set up to run Rails and create your first Rails app. Feel free to skip around.

Install Ruby

I like to use RVM to manage my rubies. I really like having project-based configurations and settings. Some languages lend themselves really well to this, and some rely more on system-wide configurations.

RVM gemsets are the perfect way to create the isolation that I like. Rails does not strictly need that isolation. `Gemfile.lock` defines gem dependencies (with versions) so that when you do have multiple versions of a gem installed it will pick the right one.

Still, there have been times when I got some gem version messed up. It was great to be able to just blow away the gemset and reinstall a clean set of gems for that app.

Once you have RVM installed and at least one ruby, you are ready to start setting up a project. The steps that I take to do that generally go like this:

```
echo 2.2.3 > .ruby-version
gem install bundler --no-rdoc --no-ri
rvm gemset create APPNAME
rvm gemset use APPNAME
gem install rails --no-rdoc --no-ri
```

I have a directory for all my projects, and I like to have that `.ruby-version` file in that directory so that whenever I change into the directory I automatically switch to the latest version of Ruby that I have installed. You can also run `rvm use 2.2.3` to change to the version manually.

Create the App

Make sure that you're still in the right gemset. You can run `rvm gemset list` to verify that. You've already installed the Rails gems, so you are ready to create the app. The steps that I generally use to create a new Rails app are:

```
rails new APPNAME --skip-bundle -d postgresql
echo 2.2.3 > APPNAME/.ruby-version
echo APPNAME > APPNAME/.ruby-gemset
cd APPNAME
git init
git add . && git commit -am'Initial commit'
```

A new Rails app is created in a subdirectory named for the project. The `.ruby-*` files tell RVM to set the version of Ruby and gemset that you want for that project. I like to do an initial commit before I start making configuration changes. The `--skip-bundle` switch tells the Rails app generator to hold off on installing any gems. Typically, the Rails generator will run `bundle install` when it's finished creating the app. We discuss this more in the next section.

The default development database is SQLite, so we have to tell Rails that we want to use Postgres. If you have options, like those, that you always want the Rails new generator to use you can put those in a configuration file in your user directory (`~/.railsrc`).

Here is my `.railsrc` file:

```
--skip-bundle
-d postgresql
```

More Gems

The reason I don't want to install the gems yet is that I have more that I want to use, and I have some that I do not want to use.

The file we need to modify is the `Gemfile`, which is in the app's root directory. Here are the modifications that I generally make:

- Add the Ruby version. Heroku needs this. RVM can use this. It also documents expectations for other developers.
- There are a lot of comments, and you don't really need them.
- Allow for minor version bumps for the Rails gem. Do this by adding ~> before the version number.
- Comment out `coffee-rails`. I do not prefer CoffeeScript.

- Add these gems:
  - `rails_12factor` (group: production)—you can omit this if you're not using Heroku
  - `dotenv-rails` (groups: development, test)
  - `puma`
  - `newrelic_rpm`
  - `lograge`

With those tweaks the Gemfile is now good enough to install some gems. Do this by running `bundle install`. That will create (or update) a `Gemfile.lock` file. Both of those files should be tracked in your source code repository.

Config Files

Now it's time to set up some of the dependencies for the app. We have a couple of things that need some configuration, like database credentials, and we have some services that we need to setup.

Puma

Puma is a multi-threaded webserver, and it's awesome. Listing A.1 shows the typical `puma` config file for Heroku. If you are using Rails 5 the Puma gem is already included.

Listing A.1 `config.puma.rb`

```
workers Integer(ENV['WEB_CONCURRENCY'] || 2)
threads_count = Integer(ENV['MAX_THREADS'] || 5)
threads threads_count, threads_count

preload_app!

rackup      DefaultRackup
port        ENV['PORT']     || 3000
environment ENV['RACK_ENV'] || 'development'

on_worker_boot do
  ActiveRecord::Base.establish_connection
end
```

New Relic

We will set this config up if/when we host. Heroku offers New Relic as an add-on, and there is a free level. You can also use New Relic on your localhost in development mode, which can be informative. Go to http://localhost:3000/newrelic as you use your app to see the dashboard.

Log Rage

This is totally optional, but once I started using it I have not stopped. You can define the format for your app logs. The configuration is done separately for each environment. The configuration that I use is below, and it goes in `config/environments/production.rb`. You can also put it in the development config file.

```
# LogRage
config.lograge.enabled = true
config.lograge.custom_options = lambda do |event|
  params = event.payload[:params].reject do |k|
    ['controller', 'action', 'format'].include? k
  end

  {
    :params => params,
    :time   => event.time.xmlschema
  }
end
```

Dot Env

Environment variables are the preferred way to tell your app about credentials. The `dotenv-rails` gem can make it easier to set these locally in development. I've also found this is a good way to document what environment variables an app depends on. Just be sure that you include `.env` in your `.gitignore`. Here is an example `.env` file with some database credentials:

```
POSTGRES_HOST=localhost
POSTGRES_USER=developer
POSTGRES_PASSWORD=password
```

Database

I like to delete the comments from the boilerplate files (`database.yml`, `routes.rb`). I also like to set myself up to use environment variables as much as possible. This makes it really easy to drop your application into a Docker container. That's where the `dot-env` gem comes into play. Listing A.2 shows my cleaned-up `config/database.yml` file.

Listing A.2 Database Config File

```
default: &default
  adapter: postgresql
  encoding: unicode
  pool: <%= ENV["DB_POOL"] || ENV['MAX_THREADS'] || 5 %>
  host: <%= ENV["POSTGRES_HOST"] || "localhost" %>
  username: <%= ENV["POSTGRES_USER"] || "developer" %>
  password: <%= ENV["POSTGRES_PASSWORD"] || "password" %>

development:
  <<: *default
  database: maryland_residential_sales_development

# Warning: The database defined as "test" will be erased and
# re-generated from your development database when you run "rake".
# Do not set this db to the same as development or production.
test:
  <<: *default
  database: maryland_residential_sales_test

production:
  <<: *default
  database: maryland_residential_sales_production
```

README

I like Markdown better than RDoc for formatting documentation, so I change the `README.rdoc` to `README.md` (`git mv README.rdoc README.md`).

Delete the boilerplate, and put in the pertinent information for the project. You should include things like the following:

- Name of the project
- Things that you are using (PostGIS would be a good thing to document)
- Steps to get the project running
- Hosting information and steps to host the project
- Anything else that someone would need to know

Finalize the Setup

Now you have all the building blocks that you need, so it's time to make sure you have all the gems installed and the database in order.

```
bundle install
bundle exec rake db:create db:migrate
git add .
git commit -am'Initial setup complete'
```

Appendix B
Brief Postgres Overview

This is a brief overview of all the little things that go into getting your environment set up to run Postgres.

Installing Postgres

Chances are your laptop or server does not have Postgres installed on it if you have not used the Postgres database before. If you're using OS X, you have the Postgres client libraries but not the database server itself.

From Source

You can download the source code for Postgres, compile it, and install it. This gives you the most control. Go to https://www.postgresql.org/ftp/source/ to download the source code. Installation instructions can be found at https://www.postgresql.org/docs/current/static/install-procedure.html.

Package Manager

If you're on a Linux distro you've got access to the Postgres and PostGIS packages in the `apt` or `yum` repos.

On OS X, Homebrew is usually my go-to tool for installing things. You can use Homebrew to install Postgres (and PostGIS). This was how I installed Postgres and PostGIS on OS X for a very long time, but it's not my preferred method now.

Postgres.app

The good people at Heroku have made an OS X application that runs the Postgres server, includes PostGIS, and has all the environmental things like header files that you need to run Postgres on OS X. This is what I use on my dev box.

SQL Tools

Once you have a database you might want to interact with it outside the scope of your application. You have a few choices for how to do that.

Command Line

I love the command line, and on a server this may be your only option. The Postgres command line client is `psql`. Here is an example of the `psql` command:

```
psql -U developer -d someapp_development -h localhost -p 5432 -W
```

Your shell username will also be the default user for `psql`, so you don't need to specify username (`-U`) unless you're using a different database user. Tell `psql` which database you want to connect to with the `-d` switch. If you are connecting to a database on the localhost you do not need to specify the host (`-h`), but it does not hurt to get in the habit of including it. The default port (`-p`) for Postgres is `5432`, so you don't need to specify that unless you're trying to access a different port. The `-W` switch is the same thing as `--password`. Both tell `psql` to ask for a password.

GUI Tool

I like two different GUI applications for interacting with a Postgres database. They both can connect to your local database(s) as well as databases in the cloud.

pgAdmin3

pgAdmin is an open source tool for Postgres. You can run pgAdmin on OS X, Linux, and Windows. The key bindings do not necessarily match up with what you might be used to for the given OS, so be aware of that.

Navicat

Navicat has several different database clients and several different versions of their apps to choose from. I like Navicat Essentials for PostgreSQL enough that I bought the license.

Bulk Importing Data

I touched on importing data in Chapter 1, "D3 and Rails," and wrote a rake task to do it one record at a time. Sometimes that is impractical. It generates a massive log file, for example, and takes a long time with large data files. There are two other choices for importing data: the `COPY` SQL statement, and the `\copy psql` command. Both require that the data line up exactly with the table, so the extra fields like `created_at` and `updated_at` will have to be dropped from the table and then added back after the data is loaded. It may also be helpful to drop all the indices on the table and add them back once the data is imported.

COPY SQL Statement

You can specify column names with this method, so you don't necessarily have to transform the data file and/or the table. The caveat here is that you cannot correct or transform any data with this method. If there are any formatting issues those have to be handled separately from the import. The file has to live on the same server as the database, though, so this option will generally not be practical in a production environment.

Nevertheless, it is a handy command to know about, especially if you're prototyping an app or just want to look at some data. Here is a hypothetical SQL statement that would copy a CSV file with headers that is located in `/usr/local/states.csv`.

```
COPY states FROM '/usr/local/states.csv' DELIMITER ',' CSV HEADER;
```

\copy PSQL Command

When you do not have access to put files on your database server but still need to import large files, you need to use the `\copy` utility. In what follows you see the same example, but in this case the file is on your local filesystem and you use the `psql` command to connect to the remote database.

```
PGPASSWORD=SEKRET psql -h 111.222.333.444 \
  -U developer \
  -d awesome_production \
  -c "\copy states FROM 'states.csv' WITH CSV HEADER;"
```

pg_restore

There is one other option that is a little higher level than bulk importing data for a table. You can export (dump) the data from a database and load it into another. The databases have to be the same version, or you have some additional hoops to jump through.

A simple `pg_restore` command that assumes you have a dump from the database that was created using the `pg_dump` command follows. Here is an example `pg_restore` for loading data to a Heroku database.

```
pg_restore --verbose --clean --no-acl --no-owner \
  -h 222.333.444.555 -U developer -d app_production \
  -p 34567 ./latest.dump
```

Listing B.1 shows a rake task that I wrote to take the data from a production Heroku database and load it into a local development database. This can also be found in a GitHub Gist at https://gist.github.com/barrettclark/c94467e3872d16b3f8b0.

Listing B.1 Load Local Database from Heroku Rake Task

```
namespace :db do
  namespace :heroku do
    desc "capture DB Backup"
    task :capture_backup => :environment do
      if Rails.env == 'development'
        Bundler.with_clean_env do
          config = Rails.configuration.database_configuration[Rails.env]
          system "heroku pg:backups capture"
        end
      end
    end

    desc "Pull DB Backup"
    task :download_backup => :capture_backup do
      if Rails.env == 'development'
        Bundler.with_clean_env do
          config = Rails.configuration.database_configuration[Rails.env]
          system "curl -o latest.dump 'heroku pg:backups public-url'"
        end
      end
    end

    desc "Load the PROD database from Heroku to the local dev database"
    task :load => :download_backup do
      if Rails.env == 'development'
        Bundler.with_clean_env do
          config = Rails.configuration.database_configuration[Rails.env]
          system <<-CMD
            pg_restore --verbose --clean --no-acl --no-owner -h localhost
➥\
              -U #{config["username"]} -d #{config["database"]}
➥latest.dump
            rm -rf latest.dump
          CMD
        end
      end
    end
  end
end
```

The Query Plan

You can see how the Postgres query optimizer thinks the most efficient way to run a query is by using the `EXPLAIN ANALYZE` command. Your local machine may not be configured the same as the production database, though, so be sure you take that into account.

Here is an example of a query used in Chapter 1:

```
EXPLAIN ANALYZE
SELECT SUM(total_sales) AS sum_total_sales, jurisdictions
FROM maryland_residential_sales_figures
GROUP BY jurisdictions

                                                               QUERY
➥PLAN
---------------------------------------------------------------
➥-----------------------------------------------------------
 HashAggregate  (cost=16.07..16.30 rows=24 width=14)
➥(actual time=1.070..1.086 rows=24 loops=1)
   Group Key: jurisdictions
   ->  Seq Scan on maryland_residential_sales_figures
(cost=0.00..13.71 rows=471 width=14) (actual time=0.064..0.256 rows=471
➥loops=1)
 Planning time: 0.190 ms
 Execution time: 1.224 ms
(5 rows)
```

When you see `seq scan`, it means that the entire table will be scanned in sequence to find the right data. If you're using fields in a `WHERE` clause, those would be good candidates for indices when you see the sequence scan.

Appendix C
SQL Join Overview

I don't know about you, but I have to look a lot of things up. There are a lot of types of joins, and I don't use most of them regularly. This appendix is really here for me, but maybe you'll find it helpful as well.

Join Example Database Setup

For this appendix I'll create a little sample database from the command line. This is completely off the rails, so to speak. You can use either the `psql` command to jump in on the command line, or you can use one of the GUI tools listed in Appendix B, "Brief Postgres Overview."

```
CREATE DATABASE join_examples;

\connect join_examples;
```

Those two lines will create an empty database and then connect to (place you in) that database. Now that we have a database we can put some sample data in it.

```
CREATE TABLE t1 (num int, name char(1));
INSERT INTO t1 VALUES (1, 'a'), (2, 'b'), (3, 'c');

CREATE TABLE t2 (num int, value char(3));
INSERT INTO t2 VALUES (1, 'xxx'), (3, 'yyy'), (5, 'zzz');
```

Inner Join

This is the default join if you do not specify `INNER` or `OUTER`. With an inner join you get all the records from both tables where the join condition is satisfied.

```
join_examples=# SELECT * FROM t1 INNER JOIN t2 USING (num);
 num | name | value
-----+------+-------
   1 | a    | xxx
   3 | c    | yyy
(2 rows)
```

That query could also be written as:

```
SELECT * FROM t1 JOIN t2 on t1.num = t2.num;
```

Left Outer Join

This is also known as a "left join." First an inner join is executed, and then all unmatched records from the table on the left side of the join are included. In the example query, `t1` is the table on the left side. I think of this as the primary table because it is the table that the query is being asked to select from. The table being joined in is the table on the right.

```
join_examples=# SELECT * FROM t1 LEFT JOIN t2 ON t1.num = t2.num;
 num | name | num | value
-----+------+-----+-------
   1 | a    |   1 | xxx
   2 | b    |     |
   3 | c    |   3 | yyy
(3 rows)
```

Right Outer Join

This is the converse of the left join and is also known as a "right join." First an inner join is executed, and then all the unmatched records from the *right* side of the join are included.

```
join_examples=# SELECT * FROM t1 RIGHT JOIN t2 ON t1.num = t2.num;
 num | name | num | value
-----+------+-----+-------
   1 | a    |   1 | xxx
   3 | c    |   3 | yyy
     |      |   5 | zzz
(3 rows)
```

Inner and left joins are the mainstay of what you will use, but it's good to know what else you have available.

Full Outer Join

This is also known as an "outer join." This gives you all the records from both tables. An inner join is executed first, and then the rest of the records are included. The values for fields in unmatched records are null.

```
join_examples=# SELECT * FROM t1 FULL JOIN t2 ON t1.num = t2.num;
 num | name | num | value
-----+------+-----+-------
   1 | a    |   1 | xxx
   2 | b    |     |
   3 | c    |   3 | yyy
     |      |   5 | zzz
(4 rows)
```

Cross Join

I don't think that I have ever used this join. It gives you every possible combination of rows from the two tables. The number of records will be the record count of `t1` * the record count of `t2`.

```
join_examples=# SELECT * FROM t1 CROSS JOIN t2;
 num | name | num | value
-----+------+-----+-------
   1 | a    |   1 | xxx
   1 | a    |   3 | yyy
   1 | a    |   5 | zzz
   2 | b    |   1 | xxx
   2 | b    |   3 | yyy
   2 | b    |   5 | zzz
   3 | c    |   1 | xxx
   3 | c    |   3 | yyy
   3 | c    |   5 | zzz
(9 rows)
```

Self Join

It may seem like a strange thing to do, but you can join a table on itself. This comes in handy when you need to compare the data in a table with itself. For example, you could list all employees for a manager (who is also an employee). You'd get the manager's name from the joined version of the table.

```
join_examples=# SELECT * FROM t2 JOIN t2 t2a USING (value);
 value | num | num
-------+-----+-----
 xxx   |   1 |   1
 yyy   |   3 |   3
 zzz   |   5 |   5
(3 rows)
```

You can see that the `num` field is brought in a second time thanks to the join. This also shows the use of a table alias, where we can give a table name (usually a long table name) an alias. This is generally a shorter, abbreviated, version of the name that we can use throughout the query to refer to that table without having the really long table name repeated and cluttering up the query.

Index

M

N

O

P

Q